Please remember that this is a library book,
and that it belongs only temporarily to each
person who uses it. Be considerate. Do
not write in this, or any, library book.

Managing
Educational Excellence

The Stanford Series on Education and Public Policy

General Editor: Professor Henry M. Levin, School of Education, Stanford University

The purpose of this series is to address major issues of educational policy as they affect and are affected by political, social and economic issues. It focusses on both the consequences of education for economic, political and social outcomes as well as the influences of the economics, political and social climate on education. It is particularly concerned with addressing major educational issues and challenges within this framework, and a special effort is made to evaluate the various educational alternatives on the policy agenda or to develop new ones that might address the educational challenges before us. All of the volumes are to be based upon original research and/or competent syntheses of the available research on a topic.

School Days, Rule Days: The Legalization and Regulation of Education *Edited by David L. Kirp, University of California, Berkeley, and Donald N. Jensen, Stanford University.*

The Incompetent Teacher: The Challenge and the Response *Edwin M. Bridges, Stanford University.*

The Future Impact of Technology on Work and Education *Edited by Gerald Burke, Monash University, Australia and Russ W. Rumberger, University of California, Santa Barbara.*

Comparing Public and Private Schools: Volume 1 Institutions and Organizations *Edited by Thomas James, Brown University and Henry M. Levin, Stanford University.*

Comparing Public and Private Schools: Volume 2 School Achievement *Edited by Edward H. Haertel, Stanford University, Thomas James, Brown University and Henry M. Levin, Stanford University.*

Managing Educational Excellence *Thomas B. Timar, Harvard Graduate School of Education and David L. Kirp, University of California, Berkeley.*

Managing Educational Excellence

Thomas B. Timar

and

David L. Kirp

 The Falmer Press

(A member of the Taylor & Francis Group)
New York • Philadelphia • London

UK The Falmer Press, Falmer House, Barcombe, Lewes, East Sussex, BN8 5DL

USA The Falmer Press, Taylor & Francis Inc., 242 Cherry Street, Philadelphia, PA 19106-1906

First published 1988

Library of Congress Cataloging in Publication Data

Timar, Thomas.
   Managing educational excellence.
   (The Stanford series on education and public policy; 6)
   Bibliography: p.
   Includes index.
   1. Education—United States—Evaluation. 2. Education and state—United States. 3. Education—United States—Aims and objectives. I. Kirp, David L. II. Title. III. Series: Stanford series on education and public policy; v. 6.
LA217.T58 1988 379.73 87-33178
ISBN 1-85000-358-0
ISBN 1-85000-359-9 (pbk.)

Jacket design by Caroline Archer

Typeset in 11/13 Bembo by
Imago Publishing Ltd, Thame, Oxon

Printed in Great Britain by Taylor & Francis (Printers) Ltd, Basingstoke

Contents

Acknowledgements

Many debts are incurred in writing a book that covers so much ground. Much of the information in this book was gathered from interviews in three states. We were fortunate in having the support and cooperation of many people in those states. We have also benefitted from the support of friends and colleagues who read chapters, directed us to new sources of information and shared their views about school reform.

We are particularly grateful to the National Institute of Education for their support at Stanford University's Institute for Research on Educational Finance and Governance. This book is the culmination of a five-year research project funded by NIE on Law and Education. This book benefits from the prior years' work, particularly the UC Berkeley-Stanford Faculty Seminars during 1980–82. Those seminars and the publications from them focused the theoretical dimensions of this book.

Colleagues and friends who provided insights and encouragement include John Shilts, Terrel Bell, Harold Hodgkinson, W. Norton Grubb and James W. Guthrie. We are particularly grateful to Douglas Mitchell and Theodore Sizer for their thorough reading of the manuscript and their extremely thoughtful and helpful comments and suggestions.

Materials for this book came from many people in California, Texas and South Carolina. They included state-level policymakers and local school administrators, teachers and parents. We are particularly indebted to the help of Terry Peterson who served as South Carolina Governor Richard Riley's education aid and to Marie Land in Manning, South Carolina who spent a day taking us to schools. Her dedication and effort to improve the quality of Manning's schools speaks much to the reform effort in the entire state.

TBT   *DLK*
San Francisco, 1987   *Berkeley, 1987*

This book is dedicated to my son, Sebastian

TBT

Preface

The 1980s will be remembered as a time of resurging interest in American schooling. This attention was long-a-coming and flowed initially from the turbulence and agonized reappraisals that followed the achievement of mass secondary education in the early 1960s and the unsettling events of the late 1960s fueled by the Civil Rights movement and the Vietnam War. A reaction to these unsettlements flowed in the 1970s, which experienced (ironically) both the achievement of Johnson's Great Society (as the vast entitlement programs ratcheted into full force) and a growing worry and skepticism about the American Way, these new worries coloring the post-Vietnam, Watergate era.

When Americans worry about themselves, they pay special attention to their schools, particularly their high schools. Public education is an American icon of sorts, and the polishing of that icon — usually expressed as 'bringing the schools back' to some earlier perfection — becomes a national fascination. Even the early, public commitments of the Reagan administration to turn away from national initiatives for education (because schooling 'was a local and state matter') were insufficient to slow down Americans' concerns about themselves and thus their schools; concerns reified in such perceptions as 'SAT score decline' and of 'unbusinesslike' educational practice.

Early in his tenure, Education Secretary Terrel H. Bell appointed a National Commission on Excellence in Education which published its celebrated and apocalyptic report 'A Nation at Risk ...' in the spring of 1983. That report merely blew on fires already smoldering and, combined with the results of several large research studies of schooling which had been initiated in the 1970s, pushed education reform and renewal to center stage, in spite of the national government's expressed disinterest in these matters.

Given the central government's tentativeness about 'doing something' about elementary and secondary education, the vacuum was filled by state government. Uniquely in American history, governors of several states put education and the reform of schools at the top of their political agendas; some ran for office on education planks. Spurred by the 1983 report, state legislatures across the country quickly enacted various 'reform packages', these in what was perceived to be a reaction to a new level of public concern. Curiously, few of these reform packages took very much account at all of the large body of new research findings that had emerged by the early 1980s, and most were driven, as always it seems in America, by the vaguely outlined icon, a simplistic vision of an earlier educational age and about how young people in fact learn.

As these reform packages came into law and, more particularly, into state regulation, their effect began to be felt in schools. In many states, these laws and regulations were indeed consequential, ones which would in time profoundly change schools, both in the specific aspects required by law but, perhaps more importantly, in the way that the public, and particularly the professionals and students, perceived their tasks to be. Those initiatives, then, could make a difference, and the way that schooling was to be perceived and pursued would be affected by them.

For these reasons an understanding of what happened with school reform in each of the states during this provocatively turbulent decade of the 1980s is of great importance. The politicization of education, the politically-perceived need to rush to various kinds of widely acceptable 'reforms', the ways and means that state leaders, charged Constitutionally for the quality and provision of education, could still respect local powers and concerns: all played out in fascinating and important ways in the five years following the issuance of that nationally important 'trigger' document, 'A Nation at Risk'. Thomas Timar and David Kirp have selected three influential states, ones which took the reform impetus seriously but which handled it in strikingly different ways. They chronicle what happened in each state by the mid 1980s and critique different approaches, taking wise account of the particularities of each state. And, in their final analysis, they raise a range of issues about 'reform' that those who would yet pursue it should take to heart.

As one reviews the Timar-Kirp chornicle and analysis, one is reminded again of how important formal schooling is for Americans, how acknowledged is the right and ritual of 'going to school' — the unchallenged acceptance of the way that schools are set forth and organized, with buildings based in localities opening after Labor Day and closing in June; with 'courses' with titles unchanged since the turn of the century; with programs that provide communities with both a source (in many cases) of local entertainment (such as Friday night basketball); and, for all, an opportunity to celebrate that most important secular Bar Mitzvah in this culture, graduation from high school. One finds little challenge in state reform efforts to these totems and, thus, is state 'reform' activity remarkably conservative; the basic institutions are largely unchallenged.

However, paradoxically, one senses too a frustration, bordering often on anger, about the inability of the traditional school to deliver on the idealistic promises which Americans have long expected the schools to meet. The purple rhetoric of 'A Nation at Risk' does express an angry longing. Responding both to stand-pat-ism and to anger, state level reform by the mid 1980s, then, takes the form of the scolding of a valued relative, an irresponsible uncle with whom one must continue to live but who is expected to shape up. There is little radical here, nothing even fainlty reminiscent of the fiery ideas of the late 1960s; the uncle is bombarded with apocalyptic rhetoric, yes; but such is accompanied only by predictable and modest, and thus unchallenging, remedies.

And so Timar and Kirp recount and critique a time of ferment, but of strikingly traditionalist ferment, a time when the discourse about schooling turned rarely away from the superficial expressions of the accepted institution, of a time where America found itself both unsure of its values but certain that it would find fresh assurance merely by strengthening that which was familiar. One sensed no new dreams, but a struggle to re-experience old ones.

One who reads the Timar-Kirp chapters is informed by what they tell us — and worries about the American imagination, and thus our future.

Theodore Sizer

1   *The New Reform Agenda*

The Transformation of Educational Policy

The decade of the 1980s has witnessed two important shifts in state education agendas. Consistent with the Reagan administration's ideological commitment to a generally reduced federal policy role in areas traditionally the responsibility of state and local governments, many educational policy decisions made primarily in Washington have devolved to state the local governments. A central theme of the Reagan administration has been deregulation of education, the desire to provide greater local decision-making consistent with local needs and preferences and, generally, to streamline educational policy implementation by stripping it of unnecessary baggage.

The commitment to a reduced federal presence in educational policy matters lay behind the early plans of the administration to dismantle the Education Department and to consolidate nearly thirty federal categorical programs into a single block grant in education. The conviction that schooling is essentially a state and local matter, not a federal concern, is further emphasized in *A Nation at Risk*, the Reagan administration's education manifesto. 'State and local officials, including school board members, governors, and legislators, have the primary responsibility for financing and governing the schools', the task force says, 'and should incorporate the reforms we propose in their educational policies and fiscal planning'.[1]

In addition to emphasizing the shift in educational policymaking and implementation to the state, *A Nation at Risk* focused attention on a new set of issues, summed as educational excellence. The idea of excellence became synonymous with the nation's capacity to survive the challenge of international economic competition. While the animating principle of federal and state education policies for the past

1

two decades has been the protection of *individuals* at risk, the new educational agenda focused on a *nation* at risk. In its souped-up prose the commission warned 'if an unfriendly power had attempted to impose on America the mediocre educational performance that exists today, we might well have viewed it as an act of war ... We have, in fact, been committing an act of unthinking, unilateral disarmament'.[2]

Reports of declining educational quality and the deterioration of the structural elements of education came in a constant stream during the Reagan administration's first term. And surveys showed that the general public viewed declining student test scores, poor teacher training and preparation, and recurring problems with student discipline with mounting concern. Education mattered to the public, but schools were not doing very well.[3] Critics of the educational system advocated various remedies to the ills of schooling: merit pay for teachers, minimum competency tests for prospective teachers, more rigorous and demanding curricula, longer school days, and stiffer high school graduation standards. All were designed to build quality into the institution.

The New Policy Culture

The Supreme Court's 1954 decision, *Brown v. Board of Education* was the genesis of two master trends in educational policy which, until the early 1980s, dominated educational policymaking.[4] Judicial elaboration of substantive rights established one trend. Its effect was to upset the traditional pattern of localist school governance dominated by school boards and professionals. Within a decade, the courts were deciding many education issues well beyond race, opening the door to a host of other rights seekers. The handicapped, the non-English speaking, ethnic minorities, and women all saw in *Brown* the opportunity to convert their victimization by local school systems into constitutional wrongs. They flooded the courts with lawsuits.

The other policy stream for which *Brown* was the wellhead established the right to formal review of official decisions, again upsetting local authority over schools. The courts extended procedural protection to many aspects of education in the 1960s. Congress adopted the judicial approach, subsequently including similar procedural guarantees for handicapped students. The reliance upon law and law-like mechanisms — legalization — became not just a judicial norm, but part of a vast regulatory regime that the federal government used to centralize much educational decision-making authority in Washington. Beginning with the 1960s, the rights of the poor and educationally disadvantaged, the handicapped, the limited English speaking, and others deemed deserving of protection were addressed through strategies that relied upon complex compliance and regulatory mechanisms.

State activity grew apace with the expanding federal presence. Many states were charged with administering federal categorical aid programs, and some federal monies were targeted to strengthening state education agencies. Other states, spurred by court decisions, sought to reform their school finance systems in order to meet the needs of special student populations, to encourage local accountability, or stimulate local experimentation. Often imitating federal strategies, the states also relied on regulatory mechanisms and strict compliance as a strategy for addressing state educational goals. Some states recognized as rights the entitlement of underserved groups to special services. California, for example, established standards and programs for handicapped students that exceeded federal requirements. Massachusetts established instructional programs for non-English speaking and limited-English speaking students that went beyond the federally prescribed *Lau* remedies. Due process guarantees for children and their parents were important components of programs serving the handicapped. State-funded categorical programs came with rigid mandates to ensure local accountability with program requirements. State reliance on regulation and compliance was a favored strategy because policy goals focused on equity, the fair allocation of education services. State education bureaucracies usually swelled in size so that the rules designed to control local behavior could be interpreted and enforced.

State programs did not always work as they were intended, however. Studies of local implementation found programs lasted only as long as there were state or federal dollars to pay for them. Categorically funded programs were rarely integrated into the regular school programs. Program funds were not always used for the purposes that policy-makers intended, and the number of rules swelled to encompass all imaginable exceptions. Regulations for the expenditure of Title I funds in California, for example, reached the absurd when they stated that monies could be used for carpeting a classroom floor only if sitting on the floor was included in the lesson plans. Money, federal money, could not be spent on carpeting if students just happened to sit on the floor, absent by pedagogical purpose.

The emergence of excellence as an educational standard forces a rethinking of implementation strategies. Excellence concerns emphasize quality of instruction rather than equalization of educational resources, content rather than allocation. Furthermore, educational excellence shifts the focus of policy to aspirations, not constitutionally protected rights, and for that reason evokes a different policy culture for its nurture. Issues of educational excellence are not expressed in the language of civil rights — the language of duty and obligations, but in the language of effective schools; they are framed in terms of what Lon Fuller has called the 'morality of aspirations'.[5] Aspirations go beyond regulation as 'there is no way that law can compel a man to live up to the excellences of which he is capable'.[6] Excellence — like aspirations generally — is not readily measured and quantified. That is why strategies which rely upon rules and mandates, accounting procedures, and compliance monitoring have little to do with attaining excellence.

The Shift from Equity to Excellence

The agenda for reform advocated in *A Nation at Risk* calls for changing standards and expectations for educational performance, improving the quality of educational professionals, and strengthening leadership in the nation's schools. There are no references to legal entitlement, no mention of federal enforcement of the report's recommendations, no ostensible issues in the report to mobilize lawyers. Implicit in the report of the National Commission on Educational Excellence is the recognition that, beyond principle, equal access has little substantive value if access is to an inferior product.

As educational policy has shifted its focus to excellence, the organizational elements of schooling — teachers, administrators, curriculum, and the learning environment — have received new attention. Though the educational policies of the 1960s and 1970s were at least nominally concerned with education, their goal was social justice. Schools were instrumental in creating a more just society in which economic wealth and political power were fairly distributed. Excellence reforms are very much school-centered and necessitate a different approach. Effective schools are the products of .a robust organizational culture whose source of strength is a shared set of attitudes, values and beliefs to develop common expectations. While institutional well-being cannot be coerced, it can be fostered. Or so the hope goes.

It does not matter how well-crafted educational policies may be or how much popular support they may enjoy if schools are incapable of turning those policies into successful programs. The goal of excellence — however loftily articulated — cannot be divorced from the institutional capacity of schools. Making mediocre state educational systems into excellent ones necessitates a policy transformation that is far more radical than anything dreamed of thus far by the states.

Implementing Excellence

According to a Department of Education report entitled *A Nation Responds,*[7] since 1983 over 300 state commissions — on average, that is six for each state — have studied the quality of their educational systems, have found them wanting, and have proposed strategies for their improvement. The report catalogues a wide array of state initiatives including, increased graduation requirements, student competency testing, and tougher teacher certification and promotion standards. According to the report, nearly each state is engaged in some type of reform activity.

The critical question that state reform efforts raise is whether reform policies yield outcomes that are consistent with standards of excellence, or whether reforms lead only to more rules, formalistic compliance, evasion, paperwork, and legal proceedings. Do reforms engender a defensive, evasive or legalistic attitude? Do schools simply turn reforms into bureaucratized routines? The avowed purpose of state reform efforts is to enhance the organizational effectiveness of schools. If schools lack the capacity to translate reforms into action, are overwhelmed with regulations, and if mandates themselves become the focus of reform efforts, the intended effect of reform policies will be lost.

Presently, there is scant experience to guide policymakers in their efforts to achieve excellence in the schools. While researchers have recognized the tangle of political, cultural, individual, and organizational factors that influence policy outcomes, few researchers have attempted to establish a causal connection between implementation choices and their effects.[8]

The tension between securing compliance and encouraging local initiative is a constant theme that runs throughout the literature on policy implementation.[9] Studies of federally funded Title I programs for the educationally disadvantaged, for example, found that local implementation was affected by so many factors as to be idiosyncratic.[10] Studies assessing the durability of education reforms found that few changes were sustained in the schools. The exceptions were structural changes. Programmatic innovations tended to dissipate over time, while structural changes, the length of the school year, for example, tended to last.[11]

State-level education reformers regularly favor policies that can be quantified — and, hence, enforced. Regulations concerning various aspects of the educational process — teacher evaluation and retention, administrative leadership, longer student seat time, standardization of the curriculum — become rough proxies for excellence. This is inevitable and may be useful for establishing a basis on which to build further reforms. The danger is that it becomes easy systematically to confuse excellence with its approximation: rigor with basics, standards for hours spent in the classroom, learning with test scores. The dilemma for policy-makers is that the most critical juncture of policy ends and means, the interaction between student and teacher, is most difficult to regulate. The fact that the most significant educational interaction may actually take place in the interstices of institutional life is a fundamental problem of educational reform.

If excellence is not wholly amenable to implementation by regulation, state policy-makers must reply on promoting styles of institutional decisionmaking that encourage professional judgment and the exercise of discretion, but in a manner consistent with policy goals. The dilemma for external reformers is to create rules for governing bureaucratic behavior without those rules becoming ends in themselves. State level education reformers, whether their intended goal is improved quality or greater equity, have a limited range of policy options for affecting school performance. State legislators may want teachers to be more dedicated and interested in their subject matter and their students, but cannot compel them to be. Love of learning and enthusiasm are qualities that cannot be coerced. The policy culture of educational excellence shifts the strategic focus from regulation and compliance to incentives and mobilization of institutional capacity. Consequently, program mandates are replaced by strategies for institutional development and policies designed to pressure unimaginative, recalcitrant and incompetent educators are replaced by strategies to empower and legitimate effective educational practices.[12]

State Implementation Strategies

State-level responses to the dilemma of state control versus local autonomy reveal fundamentally different strategies of reform and a different allocation of authority and responsibility within the state policy system. State policies vary along a continuum of control, with highly centralized policies at one extreme and decentralized policies at the other. Although this dimension of centralization is at the heart of strategic debates about policy approaches, it has received little systematic attention. Yet the issues involved are fundamental to the outcome of reform efforts. For example, the rational planning, or centralized, approach to policy implementation has been criticized for insensitivity to local needs and priorities, for demanding uniformity at the expense of innovation and diversity, and for difficulty in implementation due to the unstable nature of policy systems and the ultimate power of street-level bureaucrats.[13] Conversely, bottom-up strategies have been criticized as ineffective because they permit local official too much discretion and, thus, dilute state policy goals. The result may be balkanization of reform outcomes.

This book examines the linkage between issues of educational excellence and strategies to effect excellence in the schools. Has the educational agenda of the 1980s prompted different educational reform strategies than the rule-minded, compliance oriented model dominant during the 1960s and 1970s? When, or under what circumstances, does the social goal of equity conflict with the aspirations of educational excellence? Do reforms promoting excellence infringe upon entitlements that have been established over past twenty years? Is the culture of regulation and compliance more likely to prevail when education reforms are top-down mandates? As rules proliferate does the potential for challenge to them through litigation increase also? Does a 'bottom-up' strategy of reform promote an institutional ethos conducive to school improvement as opposed to a cafeteria of reform policies?

The questions focus on two critical dimensions of reform: substance and strategy. The substance of school reforms enacted by the states falls into four general areas. The first area focuses on efforts to improve the teaching profession by tightening standards for licensure, finding incentives to keep superior teachers in the classroom, making it easier to weed out poor and incompetent teachers, and attracting able people to teaching. The second area focuses on improving the learning environment. Reforms here generally include better use of class time; extending instructional time; strict student discipline codes; and restrictions on participation in extra-curricular activities. The third area of improvement encompasses efforts to strengthen curriculum standards and student proficiency. Competency and basic skills testing, core curricula, special programs, and increased college en-

7

trance requirements are typical strategies. The final and fourth area is in school leadership. Most often this includes honing the competencies of school administrators.

Chapter 2 describes the substantive dimensions of the reforms that states have adopted in their pursuit of educational excellence. It examines how states define educational excellence and specific policies states have adopted to achieve it. It discusses the assumptions that animate various reform policies and discusses various themes associated with educational reform policies among the states.

Chapter 3 assesses the inherent dilemma of regulating for excellence. It traces reform policies as they move through the educational bureaucracy and illustrates how the intent of reforms, encouraging educational excellence, may often be twisted to conform to local needs.

Chapter 4 concerns the strategic dimension of reform. It describes three distinct state strategies to change state school systems. These strategies may be viewed along a continuum. 'Technocratic', 'top-down' strategies based upon a business-industrial model are at one end of this continuum and 'negotiated, bottom-up' strategies at the other. Between the extremes is a negotiated, *laissez-faire* implementation strategy. The three case studies of Texas, South Carolina, and California exemplify implementation strategies along this continuum.

Chapter 5 develops a theoretical framework for assesssing educational reform strategies and relates state reform strategies to outcomes. It assesses the potential for achieving excellence in the schools. The focus is primarily on the relationship between reform policies and institutions. Specifically, this chapter examines how far policies reach to create the organizational conditions that foster educational excellence.

The lesson to be drawn from twenty years of federal and state reform efforts is that disparate reform policies have minimal lasting, beneficial effect on schools. To the contrary, schools have been so bombarded with external demands that they have disintegrated as organizations. Twenty years of reforms — collective bargaining, compensatory education, bilingual education, student rights, accountability, back-to-basics, busing, school prayer, to name a few — have transformed schools into amoeba-like institutions, they respond to a variety of external stimuli, but effect no action on their own.

Notes and References

1. The National Commission on Excellence in Education *A Nation at Risk: The Imperative for Educational Reform*, (April, 1983) page 33. Emphasis added.
2. *Ibid.*, page 5.
3. 'Survey of Education', *Phi Delta Kappan* (September, 1982).
4. See David L. Kirp 'The Fourth R: Reading, 'riting, 'rithmetic — and rules' in David L. Kirp and Donald R. Jensen (Eds). *School Days, Rules Days*, (London: Falmer Press, 1986)
5. Lon Fuller *The Morality of Law*, (New Haven: Yale University Press 1964)
6. *Ibid.*, page 9.
7. US Department of Education *The Nation Responds: Recent Efforts to Improve Education*, (Washington, DC: Government Printing Office, 1984)
8. See Richard Elmore 'Organizational models for social program implementation', *Public Policy*, 26 (1978); 'Backward mapping: Implementation research and policy implementation', *Political Science Quarterly*, 94 (1979–80). Also Larry Cuban 'Transforming the frog into a prince: Effective schools research, policy, and practice at the district level', *Harvard Education Review* 54 (1984); Guy Benveniste 'Implementation and intervention strategies', in David L. Kirp and Donald Jensen (Eds) *School Days, Rule Days* (London: Falmer. 1986); Paul Berman 'From compliance to learning: Implementing legally induced reforms', in David L. Kirp and Donald Jensen, (Eds) *School Days, Rule Days*, (London: Falmer. 1986); Paul Berman and Milbery W. McLaughlin *Federal Programs Supporting Educational Change: Vol. VII* (Santa Monica, CA: Rand Corp., 1978); Eugene Bardach *The Implementation Game* (Cambridge, Mass: MIT Press 1977). Jeffrey Pressman and Aaron Wildavsky *Implementation* (Berkely: University of California Press 1973); Aaron Wildavsky *Speaking Truth to Power: The Art and Craft of Policy Analysis* (Boston: Little, Brown and Co. 1979).
9. The problem is not limited to education. Many policymakers have watched the intent of their well-crafted programs twisted into shapes congenial to local needs. Pressman and Wildavsky subtitle their study on implementation *How Great Expectations in Washington Are Dashed in Oakland; Or, Why It's Amazing that Federal Programs Work at All, This Being a Saga of the Economic Development Corporation as Told by Two Sympathetic Observers Who Seek to Build Morals on a Foundation of Ruined Hopes.*
10. See Berman and McLaughlin.
11. John W. Meyer, W. Richard Scott, David Strang, and Andrew Creighton *Bureaucratization without Centralization: Changes in the Organizational System of American Public Education, 1940-1980*, (Stanford: Institute for Research on Educational Finance and Governance, August 1985)
12. Ibid.
13. See Robert Gerstein 'The practice of fidelity to the law', in Samuel Krislov *et al. Compliance and the Law: A Multi-Disciplinary Approach*

(Beverly Hills, CA: Sage Publications, 1972). See also Richard Weatherly and Michael Lipsky 'Street-level bureaucrats and institutional innovation: Implementing special education reform', *Harvard Education Review*, 47 (May, 1977).

2   Elements of Reform

The States Respond

Since the release of *A Nation at Risk*, education has risen dramatically on the policy agendas of many states. Over thirty other national reports on education, more than 300 state commissions and blue ribbon task force reports, several television documentaries, countless professional journals, magazine and newspaper articles have sought to shed light on the nation's educational malaise. Some of these efforts had begun earlier, but the reports turned a spotlight on state education systems. The magnitude and rapidity of state action make it virtually impossible to keep abreast of developments. While state responses differ dramatically, from the marginal to the purportedly comprehensive, nearly every state has done something.

As states seek to reform their educational systems, new players have emerged as leaders in the movement toward educational excellence. Business groups and state level politicians, particularly governors, have assumed an active role in promoting educational reform as well as securing additional state tax dollars to pay for them. For example, Tennessee's governor, Lamar Alexander, anticipated spending 80 per cent of his working hours in 1985 promoting educational reform. When the governor sought reelection in 1982, he ran on a platform 'promising a reversal of a long history of poorly financed schools, low teacher salaries, and high student dropout rates'.[1] In New York, Governor Mario Cuomo proposed spending $60 million to increase teacher salaries, $26 million to buy computers, and $1 million for competitive planning grants to districts that wish to develop specialized high schools like the Bronx High School of Science or Stuyvesant High School in New York City. South Carolina's

Governor Richard Riley devoted nearly one year to meetings with business leaders and parents' groups in order to develop support for the state's comprehensive educational reform package. Governors in Minnesota, California, Virginia, Arkansas, Texas, Mississippi, Georgia, North Carolina and Florida have pushed and prodded their legislatures to enact an array of reform policies.

In some states, business groups have been very visible participants in school reform efforts. The California Business Roundtable commissioned a study of the state's school system. Findings from that study, which were highly publicized, found their way into California's comprehensive reform package. After the reform package was enacted in Senate Bill 813, the Business Roundtable supported research to monitor the effects of reform.[2] In Texas, businessman H. Ross Perot was the driving force behind reform. He chaired the committee which developed reform proposals and hired his own political lobbyists to promote their legislative enactment. In South Carolina the involvement of business groups was a critical element not only for passage of the state's comprehensive reform package that included a one cent sales tax earmarked for education, but also for assuring continuity of the reform effort.

Some states simply accelerated existing efforts to improve their school systems. The roots of reform are evident, for example, in state efforts to equalize funding among schools, cost containment movements such as California's Proposition 13, and the 'back-to-basics' movement. New York and California initiated school improvement programs during the 1970s that encouraged local school personnel and parents to improve the quality of instructional offerings. Shifts in the traditional pattern of state-local finance concentrated policy making at the state level. In 1960, nationally, approximately 60 per cent of public school revenues came from local sources. By 1982, the proportion of the local contribution had slipped to 45 per cent.[3] In addition to changing funding patterns, states were spurred to action by increasing media attention to sagging student SAT scores, horror stories about school violence, and mounting evidence of poorly trained and unqualified teachers. Solving these problems was either beyond the capacity of local districts or beyond their policy jurisdiction.

Even though the trend toward increased state responsibility in education was evident, it is doubtful that anyone could have predicted, prior to 1980, the wave of reform that would sweep over the states. Moreover, few would have predicted the change in state-local relations that the excellence reforms have engendered.

Table 1   Major State Reform Initiatives

Reform	Enacted	Under Consideration	Total
Career ladder/merit pay	14	24	38
Salary increase/new minimum	18	17	35
Teacher testing	29	10	39
Revise certification	28	16	44
Revise teacher training	19	10	29
Aid prospective teachers	24	13	37
Add instructional time	13	7	20
Restrict extra-curricular activities	6	4	10
Reduce class size	13	7	20
Raise graduation requirements	43	5	48
Require exit test	15	4	19
Statewide assessment	37	6	43
Test for promotion	8	3	11
Increase college admission requirements	17	3	20
Academic recognition programs	25	5	30
Academic enrichment programs	34	8	42
State mandated discipline policy	19	8	27
Professional development for teachers	30	14	44
Professional development for administrators	30	12	42

Source: US Department of Education; *Education Week* (2 June 1984)

Elements of Reform

While states have enacted a bewildering array of policy intitiatives, no coherent vision of educational excellence emerges from the states. The objectives of school reform are defined by discrete programs. State policymakers assume, obviously, that if the various program objectives are realized, educational excellence follows. However, there is no definition of excellence, no concept of what excellent schools, as institutions should look like.

Generally, state reform efforts fall into five categories: (1) the teaching profession; (2) school organization and environment; (3) curriculum and academic standards; (4) administration and leadership; (5) funding. This clustering of reform initiatives represents a convenient way of clustering related actions for analysis. Over a dozen states have enacted comprehensive reform measures; that is, they have taken action in each of these categories. Virtually all states have taken some action in at least one, and often more, of these areas. Table 1 shows major state actions as of 1984.

The Teaching Profession

Teachers are central to the educational enterprise. Theodore Sizer, Chair of Brown University's Department of Education, argues in his discussion of school reform that:

> An imaginative, appropriate curriculum placed in an attractive setting can be unwittingly smothered by journeymen instructors. It will be eviscerated by incompetents. On the other hand, good teachers can inspire powerful learning in adolescents, even under the most difficult circumstances.[4]

While there may be agreement on the importance of teaching, the teaching profession itself has come under a barrage of criticism in the past five years. Increasingly, school personnel perceived themselves to be working in an atmosphere of criticism, declining confidence and support, and little appreciation. The National Commission on Excellence also concluded that:

> not enough of the academically able students are being attracted to teaching; that teacher preparation programs need substantial improvement; that the professional working life of teachers is on the whole unacceptable ...[5]

SAT scores of prospective teachers have been the lowest of any profession. The average prospective teacher scores in the bottom quartile of the SAT examination. Between 1976 and 1981, Graduate Record Examination scores of prospective teachers plummeted from 39 to 65 points below the national average. Among twenty-nine fields of study, students in teacher training programs ranked 26th on standardized tests of basic achievement. The California State University system, which prepares 65 per cent of teachers trained in that state, found in 1983 that 40 per cent of its student teachers could not pass a test of basic skills in reading, writing, and arithmetic. The failure rate at one college was 67 per cent.[6] Anecdotal evidence pointed to teachers who could not spell, compose a sentence, or compute. Critics began to wonder aloud whether teacher training programs, credentialing requirements, and certification imposed any standards at all or simply acted as pass-through agents.

Working conditions in schools are hardly the kind to attract the best and the brightest to teaching. Teachers are often isolated in the classroom, 'which becomes a teacher's total world. It is a world that is unique and separate from the world of other adults. For six hours each day, five days a week, teachers live in an exclusive and totally controlled environment'.[7] Contact with other adults during the school day is generally minimal, limited to a few minutes before and after school or during lunch break. In elementary school, even that amount of adult interaction may be impossible as teachers are often required to eat with their students in the school cafeteria. Not only do teachers have little control over working conditions, they also have little professional autonomy. They rarely select the classes they will teach — sometimes teachers receive entirely new teaching assignments only a few weeks before the start of school — or the materials with which to teach them.

Good teachers are difficult to attract and even more difficult to keep. For every new math teacher who is recruited, thirteen leave teaching. In the past ten years, public school teaching has suffered a greater loss of prestige than any other profession. Parents no longer encourage their children to enter teaching; enrollments in teacher preparation programs have declined; and more than 40 per cent of those currently employed as teachers say they would not opt to enter the profession if they could chose again.[8] Only 40 per cent of new teachers remain in the profession after five years in the job.[9]

In addition to less than ideal working conditions and low professional status, teaching salaries are generally lower than those in other professions. The Carnegie Foundation found that average starting salaries for teachers with bachelors degrees in 1981–82 was $12,769. By contrast, for engineers with similar educational attainment, it was $22,368, and for computer scientists it was $20,364.[10] In California the average teacher earns approximately $22,755 annually, 20 per cent less than a social worker and 40 per cent less than an engineer.[11]

States have recently been making extensive efforts to strengthen the teaching profession and make entry more attractive. Strategies to that end include: tightening standards of entry into the teaching profession, increasing beginning salaries for teachers, creating career ladders, instituting performance based pay schemes, providing inservice training and incentive grants, financing summer programs and institutes, particularly in science and mathematics, and scholarships for high achieving undergraduate students who make a commitment to teaching.

Proficiency Tests

Increasing numbers of states require prospective teachers to pass basic proficiency tests as a condition for receiving a credential. Such tests are intended to keep those who failed to achieve minimum competency in basic skills out of teaching. Texas, for example, requires a basic skills entry test for admission to teacher credential programs. In Texas and Arkansas, all teachers, regardless of how long they have taught, are required to pass a basic skills and subject area test. Tennessee also insists that students entering state programs pass a basic skills and composition test, while graduates of teacher education programs must pass both a basic skill and subject mastery test. In addition, Tennessee state law allows the state board of education to revoke a college's right to license teachers if over 30 per cent of its students fail to pass the required tests in two consecutive years. In California prospective teachers cannot be licensed without first passing a basic skills test.

A test of basic skills will screen out those who are incompetent, but it does not establish a very high standard for teacher performance. Those who pass such tests may know the fundamentals of reading and writing, but the tests do not reveal whether they know anything more.

The popularity of testing is largely attributable to the fact that the tests are draped in a mantle of objectivity. Quantifiable standards are readily grasped by the public and are easily defended by state policy makers on that ground. It is easy to argue that prospective or currently employed teachers who lack basic academic skills are obstacles on the road to educational excellence.

Despite the apparent appeal of this approach, significant problems have surfaced. In some Texas schools of education, particularly those with high ethnic minority enrollments, the failure rate on basic skills tests in quite high. One state official believes that some colleges would have their entire departments of education virtually eliminated by high failure rates. In 1985 Mexican-American Legal Defense Education Fund (MALDEF) unsuccessfully attempted to amend legislation in an effort to eliminate what the organization claimed was on unfair cultural bias. One provision of the proposed legislation would have required cutting those questions that fewer than 40 per cent of all candidates taking the examination or fewer than 40 per cent of any racial or ethnic group answer correctly. Also eliminated would be questions for which the correct answer rate of any two racial or ethnic groups differed by more than 10 percentage points.[12] While MALDEF was unsuccessful in legislative enactment of these provisions, the organization has had greater success in the courts.[13] MALDEF has successfully challenged in the federal circuit court the state mandated test for prospective teachers.[14] The trial court enjoined schools of education from barring admission to students who failed the test. The

Fifth Circuit Court dissolved the preliminary injunction and has sent the matter back to the trial court. The issue is far from resolved.

The teacher proficiency tests that have received the greatest publicity are those which test all teachers, regardless of years of teaching experience and quality of prior evaluation. In Texas and Arkansas, teachers and administrators must pass a basic skills test and a subject area test to retain their professional certification. In Arkansas teachers may opt to complete six graduate credits with a minimum grade of B in their teaching areas in lieu of taking the test. Arkansas teachers threatened, but did not carry out, a boycott of the test. In Texas, the largest teachers' union, the Texas State Teachers Association, has filed in federal district court to block the dismissal of teachers who failed the basic competency test. The union argues that the test discriminates against members of minority groups. Black teachers and administrators failed the test at a rate 17 percentage points above the failure rate for whites.[15]

How the issue of teacher competency testing fares in the courts will depend upon several factors. Chief among them is the number of teachers who pass the test. A high failure rate, especially among ethnic minorities, would naturally prompt a larger number of challenges.[16] Legal challenges to pre-professional tests in Texas and Alabama, for example, are based on disparities between the passing rates of minorities and non-minorities. Another issue that may wind up the courts is the relationship between professional evaluation and testing. In both Texas and Arkansas, teachers who fail the professional competency test lose their teaching credentials regardless of their past performance. A history of satisfactory teaching performance is secondary to performance on a basic skills test. Something is unreliable — either the evaluation or the test. Either prior appraisals were grossly inaccurate, in which case evaluation itself becomes suspect; or satisfactory teaching is unrelated to knowledge of basic skills, in which case teaching itself becomes suspect; or the test inaccurately measures a person's knowledge of basic skills, in which instance the test is suspect.

The cost of testing is also no small matter. Texas officials estimate that the price tag for a teacher proficiency test may be as high as $1 million. A regular evaluation process might be a more reliable and less costly measure of a teacher's mastery of basic skills. If evaluation fails to discover major deficiencies in a teacher's academic preparation, it is doubtful that testing for basic skills could adequately compensate for such a failure. The logic of testing for basic competencies suggests a direct correlation between teaching competence and knowledge of basic skills as demonstrated by passing a test. But if a teacher's competence is not evident from regular evaluation, then it is the evaluation process that is in need of repair. The policy goal of screening incompetent teachers from the profession might be more effectively accomplished through strengthened evaluation processes.

Performance or Incentive Based Pay[17]

Several strategies — including the career ladder, master and mentor teacher, merit pay for teachers and merit schools (incentive money that goes to schools for improved student performance) — are designed to reward superior teachers. Whatever they are called, most incentive based pay plans contain very similar provisions. Generally, they embody some variation of pay-for-performance. The aim of career ladders and merit pay is to provide incentives to teachers to excel and to make salary not exclusively a function of numbers of course credits and years of teaching amassed. Neither longevity nor numbers of college credits has been positively related to teaching effectiveness.

Merit pay schemes give monetary rewards to teachers for outstanding performance. Performance is typically based upon professional evaluation. No additional duties are required of the teacher to receive the stipend. Florida's Master Teacher Program and District Quality Incentive Program, enacted by the legislature in 1984, was a comprehensive program that intended to pay teachers for successful teaching. Under the Master Teacher Program, teachers could qualify for master teacher status with four years of teaching experience, two of them in Florida; a master's degree in an appropriate field, a certificate of vocational training, or attaining of a superior score on a prescribed subject matter examination; and superior teaching performance based upon evaluation by the school principal and an outside observer. Approximately 5 per cent (about 6000) of Florida's teachers were qualified. Those selected received a $3000 bonus at the end of the year and could continue to receive the bonus for three years without being reevaluated. Under the District Quality Instruction Program, local districts could qualify for state funding for merit pay for teachers. Districts developed plans for awarding bonuses. Awards could be to all teachers in a particular school or to those teachers whose students showed extraordinary gains in academic achievement or to those teachers who taught in areas where there was a critical shortage of teachers.

In contrast to incentive pay, a master or mentor teacher receives extra pay for assuming extra duties and responsibilities. Those responsibilities may include supervision of interns or curriculum development. Teachers are generally selected on the basis of outstanding performance. California's mentor teacher program is available for five per cent of the state's teachers. Those selected serve for three years, after which they may be selected longer or return to their previous status. Washington state has also established a mentor teacher program which is intended to assist beginning teachers through supervision by an experienced teacher. The mentor teachers — 100 in the first year — receive a stipend for the additional supervisory work.

The career ladders is perhaps the most popular strategy for rewarding teaching excellence and encouraging teachers to remain in the profession. There is considerable variation among states in program design and implementation, from Texas' highly prescriptive state mandated program as enacted to Utah's highly discretionary, locally developed programs.[18]

Utah provided $18 million in state funding for districts to voluntarily develop career ladders in 1985 and an additional $23 million (roughly $2000 per teacher) in 1986. All forty of the state's school districts chose to participate. The career ladder advancement provisions, which provide salary boosts and higher status for selected teachers, have spurred considerable innovation in evaluation. To date, two-thirds of Utah's districts have revised their evaluation practices. In some districts, criteria for placement on the ladder are quite subjective, while in others placement depends more upon quantifiable data. According to state education officials, most districts have begun using evaluation committees — sometimes comprised of peers — as well as administrators who historically handled evaluation matters. A teacher's rating now may include student progress. Teachers who have been promoted on the career ladders are used to revise the curriculum and to help train new teachers.

Tennessee's career ladder plan is one of the most comprehensive. The state's ladder consists of five rungs. Beginning with a 'probationary teacher' rank — a one-year appointment, followed by promotion to the second rung or dismissal — teachers proceed to the apprentice level and can eventually become Career Level III teachers. A Career Level III teacher can earn bonuses ranging from $1000 to $7000, depending upon the length of the teaching contract. During 1984–85, 90 per cent, or approximately 37,000, of Tennessee's teachers elected to participate in the career ladder. Participating teachers received a $1000 salary bonus. Another 1,080 teachers qualified for the second rung of the career ladder. Teachers are evaluated at the local level while at the first rung; state evaluations are required for subsequent steps.[19]

While teacher participation in Tennessee's career ladder program is purely voluntary, the program itself is characterized by a high degree of standardization and uniformity. Placement criteria, evaluation standards — including who conducts the evaluations and qualifications of the evaluators — retention on the career ladder; extra duties and length of service are all prescribed in the law.

During debate leading to its enactment, California's Mentor Teacher Program was billed as extra pay for extra work, to make it politically more palatable. But recipients of the extra pay are selected on the basis of 'exemplary teaching ability.'[20] The program offers state funded stipends for up to 5 per cent of the permanent classroom teachers in California. Mentor teachers are nominated by committees comprised of a majority of classroom teachers, with local school boards making the final selection. Mentors receive a $4000 bonus for extra duties, including providing assistance and guidance to both new and experienced teachers, and offering staff or curriculum development assistance. Yet, mentors are teachers first, so must spend at least 60 per cent of their time in 'direct instruction of students'.

Financial Incentives

Even as declining test scores, functional illiteracy and poorly prepared high school and college students all pointed to the failure of public schools, teachers often came to regard themselves as scapegoats for failures beyond their control. Because they feel misunderstood, underpaid, unappreciated, and asked to bear responsibility for problems which defy resolution, many of the most promising teachers leave teaching for more rewarding work. Those who are most motivated and show greatest promise as college students are usually the first to leave. In addition, women, who thirty years ago provided a ready pool of teachers, increasingly pursued careers in fields that formerly were closed to them. This fact, coupled with the loss of prestige enjoyed by the teaching profession, has made it difficult to attract highly competent individuals to the teaching profession. Consequently, states are searching for incentives to attract those individuals to teaching who would otherwise be lost to other professions. The most common strategies are to provide financial incentives to students — particularly students in areas where teaching shortages exist — to become teachers. Specific strategies to that end generally fall into three categories: increasing salaries for beginning teachers, scholarship and loan forgiveness programs for prospective teachers, and alternatives to the traditional certification process.

Beginning salaries for teachers lag far behind beginning salaries in other professions: they have been about half of starting salaries for graduates in engineering, computer science, or business. Students who possess strong skills in math or science are not likely to enter a profession that pays a starting salary of $12,000 when they can earn $25,000 in another field. This is why a number of states have increased base salaries for all teachers and have increased beginning teachers' salaries. Hoping to attract new teachers with higher entry-level salaries, California subsidizes beginning teacher salaries up to $18,000 per year over a three year period, while Texas has increased salaries for new teachers by establishing a state floor of $15,200. Other states have acted to increase base salaries for all teachers through state subsidy. Arkansas raised salaries by $1650, bringing the state average for all teachers to $17,350. Tennessee boosted teachers' salaries by 10 per cent across-the-board increase. South Carolina provided districts with a $60 million state subsidy to bring all teachers' salaries to the South-eastern average in 1984–85; while Alabama has increased teachers' base salaries by 15 per cent to $20,000; Kansas increased salaries by 9.75 per cent, and North Carolina by 14.8 per cent.[21] Georgia requires beginning salaries of teachers to be comparable to beginning salaries in comparable private sector jobs.

In an effort to attract potential teachers who have not taken the usual teacher training courses, some states offer alternatives to traditional credentialing routes. New Jersey's solution is unique among the states. To be eligible for employment as a provisional teacher in New Jersey, a candidate must hold a bachelor's degree in an appropriate major and pass a state subject-matter test. The alternative training program includes 200 hours of instruction in areas such as classroom management, effective teaching, and child development. Of the 200 hours of training, 80 hours must be completed before the candidate is allowed to take charge of a classroom, while the remaining 120 hours is taken during the first years as a closely supervised new teacher. Formal instruction for the provisional teachers is provided by college faculty members and qualified public school personnel at regional centers coordinated by the state department of education. Alternative credential programs are offered in local districts approved by the department. Each teaching candidate also spends one month under the supervision of an experienced teacher before assuming full responsibility in the classroom.

During the first ten weeks in charge of a class, the provisional teacher is observed each week. Observations are conducted by a team comprised of the school principal, an experienced teacher, a curriculum supervisor, and a college professor. Provisional teachers are observed monthly in the following 20 weeks. Finally, school principals recommend whether teaching candidates should receive standard teaching credentials.[22] By the end of June, 1985, approximately 1000 prospective teachers had applied for the alternate certification, and 56 of the state's 600 school districts are also participating. California allows school districts with shortages in critical areas to hire non-credentialed teachers who have a bachelor's degree in the subject they will teach, who have received a passing score on basic skills and subject area tests, and who agree to work with a master teacher.

Some states provide a combination of financial incentives to prospective teachers through tuition reimbursement of low interest loans which may be forgiven for years of teaching service. Washington, for example, provides forgivable loans for teaching candidates in mathematics and science. New York also provided $2 million to establish scholarships and a loan-forgiveness program to attract mathematics and science students into the teaching profession; North Carolina has increased the number of its scholarship loans to recruit top college students by providing them with a maximum of $8000 in forgivable financial aid; Tennessee, South Carolina, and Mississippi have established similar programs.

Incentive Grants and Special Academies

The daily isolation of teachers from the adult world and the routine and repetition of teaching effectively conspire against a collegial exchange of ideas, practices, and experiences. Under such circumstances, teaching practices tend to become stale, ideas and experiences are lost in isolation, exposure to innovation and new ideas is all but impossible.[23] To give teachers some intellectual stimulation, collegial contact with other adults — particularly in specialized fields outside of teaching — and to encourage an exchange of effective teaching practices, some states have adopted entirely new approaches.

New Jersey proposed grants of up to $15,000 for teachers who develop effective teaching methods. The California legislature appropriated $17.1 million for the 1984–85 school year for instructional improvement programs, enabling teachers or groups of teachers to receive stipends up to $2000. Those stipends are supposed to encourage teacher innovation and research into effective instructional practices. Other states, Kentucky and Virginia among them, have funded summer institutes for mathematics and science teachers. These programs are principally aimed at improving teaching skills in special areas, particularly for teachers who lack specific training in mathematics, science, and computers. And a number of states, including Minnesota, Missouri, and Nebraska, also provide money for regular inservice training. At the beginning of 1985, 30 states had enacted programs to provide some form of teacher inservice training.

A variation of inservice training that is intended to stimulate teacher contact with professionals in specialized areas is those programs which provide teachers with private sector jobs. Participants in these programs are most often teachers of math, science or computer use and are employed for a summer or, in some instances, perhaps for as long as a year. This type of program is available to teachers in California, Virginia, and North Carolina.

The Learning Environment

In a study of inner city London schools, researchers sought to identify what made superior schools superior. The research team found, unsurprisingly, that there were distinct differences among schools in their capacity to promote positive academic achievement.[24] The literature of effective schools also argues for differences among schools and identifies a host of variables that influence a school's learning environment.[25] The common thread in the research on effective schools is captured by the concept of 'school ethos'. Ethos encapsules a range of institutional factors: the nature and content of the curriculum; the quantity and quality of time spent in school; the attitudes of teachers and administrators toward learning; and, generally, the quality of the academic experience.

In its appraisal of schooling in America, the Commission on Excellence noted the fact that American students tend to spend much less time engaged in school work than their counterparts in other nations. Moreover, the time that is spent in the classroom and on homework is spent ineffectively.[26] Among its recommendations, the commission urged better classroom management, more effective organization of the school day, more stringent homework policies, and more effective use of teacher time by reducing their clerical responsibilities. Other critics have pointed to the fact that the length of the school day and school year is shorter in the United States than in other countries, particularly Japan.[27] Echoing similar concerns, the

Task Force on Education and Economic Growth exhorted state governments to restore the integrity of classroom instruction. Specifically, it noted that:

> ... states and local school systems should also consider lengthening the school year and the school day and extending teachers' contracts. Learning time should be increased, moreover, by establishing a wider range of learning opportunities beyond the normal school day and school year: summer institutes and after-school enrichment programs sponsored by business, for example.[28]

In addressing the Texas legislature as it began its deliberations on school reform, H. Ross Perot repeatedly emphasized the need to 'recapture the school day'. Anyone who has spent much time in an average public high school knows that teaching competes with myriad activities which in some way infringe upon instructional time. Pep rallies, assemblies, spirit week, beauty contests and the like seem to have become fixed features of education. When a high school football team leaves school early to travel to another city, a team of trainers, cheerleaders and song girls is generally in attendance. Then there is always track, basketball, baseball, field hockey, tennis, swimming, badminton, golf, drama, forensics, and so on. Finally, there are student work schedules, which in the senior high schools and particularly in the last two years, are accommodated by adjusting class schedules.

States have responded variously to criticisms of institutional flaccidity in their schools. A number of states have lengthened the school day as well as the school year. Others have enacted state policies regarding student participation in extra-curricular activities, use of instructional time, student discipline, homework, and attendence.

Increasing Instructional Time

Most states have increased instructional time in their schools. Specific policies are aimed at extending the school day, the school year, or increasing the number of hours spent on instruction. In 1983, the average number of instructional days for all the states was 178 days, with a range from 173 to 180 and with just over half the states at the latter number.[29]

California's school reform legislation offers school districts two incentives to increase instructional time. The first provides $35 per average daily attendance (ADA) to districts that offer a 180–day school year. The measure leaves unchanged the statutory minimum school year of 175 school days. If a school district offered a 180–Day program in 1983–84, it was not obligated to add any additional days of instruction to qualify for incentive funds. All that was required is that the 180–day school year be offered in 1984–85. If a district's school year falls below 180 days in any subsequent year, the $35 per ADA is lost in that year. The measure's second incentive encourages districts to increase the total instructional time offered to their students over a three-year period by providing additional funds if certain target levels of instruction are met. While districts are not required to participate in the program, it gives each district an addition $20 per ADA for grades K–8 and $40 per ADA for grades 9–12 if the district increases the total instructional time. The plan provides for cumulative funding adjustments over a three-year period, resulting in $60 or $120 per ADA to districts who voluntarily comply. The cost of the two programs, over the year, was $250 million.

North Carolina is also experimenting with a longer school day and year. The state initiated a three-year pilot project, commencing in 1983–84 in two counties. Students in the two county districts attend school thirty minutes more daily and for ten months instead of nine. Teachers also work an additional month — eleven months instead of ten.[30] The cost to North Carolina to support these programs is $2 million annually. Kentucky now requires a six-hour instructional day and a 175-day instructional year; and the legislature specified that the time must be spent solely for instruction. South Carolina increased its academic year from 185 to 190 days to give teachers five additional days for planning and preparation. The state also increased the school day to six hours, exclusive of a lunch period. Days missed for inclement weather must be made up.

A number of states have elected simply to extend the school day. Louisiana, for example, lengthened the school day to six hours for all of its students. Arkansas increased the instructional day from five to five and one-half hours, while Indiana requires five hours of instruction in grades K–6 and six hours of instruction in grades 7–12. Delaware has added thirty minutes daily for grades 1 and 2; and Florida added an additional period to the high school day.

Mandatory Attendance

Mississippi began requiring compulsory school attendance beginning with the 1983–84 school year, the last state to do so. The requirement is to be phased in over a six-year period. Arkansas increased the age when students may voluntarily leave school from 16 to 17 and requires school attendance beginning with age seven. And Arizona raised the mandatory attendence level for its students from the eighth to the tenth grade.

Reduced Class Size

Large class sizes necessarily limit the individual attention that teachers may devote to their students. The problem is particularly critical in the upper grades — mainly 9 through 12 — where students have a different teacher for each subject. Under those circumstances it is impossible to spend more than a few minutes daily with each student. That is what has motivated state policymakers to reduce the number of students in classes.

Arkansas' reform measure establishes average pupil teacher ratios for kindergarten at 20 to 1; for grades 1–6 at 25 to 1; and in grades 7–12, teachers may not exceed 150 students daily and may not have more than thirty pupils in a class with the exception of courses such as band and physical education. While the law allows some flexibility, it also fixes absolute limits on the number of students that may be assigned to a classroom.[31] Indiana's Project Prime Time began as a pilot program in nine districts to study the effects of reduced class size in the elementary grades. In 1984, the state expended $19 million to reduce student teacher rations in K–3, to be fully effective by 1990.[32] Texas has placed an absolute limit of twenty-two pupils in grades K–2 beginning in 1985–86 and 3–4 in 1988–89.

Student Attendance

The frequency of student absences from school has concerned policymakers in a number of states. Both Texas and South Carolina limit the number of days that students may be absent from classes. Texas law forbids giving a student credit for a class if the student has five or more days of unexcused absence during a semester. Furthermore, local boards of trustees must recommend for disciplinary action any student who accrues more than five days of unexcused absence during a semester or more than ten days during the school year. South Carolina, on the other hand, requires the state board of education to establish regulations definding lawful and unlawful absences beyond those specified in legislation. Districts must take action when a student has three consecutive unlawful absences or a total of five unlawful absences.

Extra-curricular Activities

Several states have established 'no pass, no play' rules governing student participation in various extra-curricular or co-curricular activities, including sports, music, and drama, as well as various club activities that focus on social or academic interests. While such activities have traditionally been an integral part of schools, many educators believe that student participation in extra-curricular activities threatens to eclipse instruction.

Several states, Florida, West Virginia, Texas, South Carolina among them, restrict student participation in extra-curricular activities for academic reasons. In Texas, a student who receives a grade lower than seventy in any class, must be suspended from participation in any extra-curricular activities during the next grade reporting period. Students who are eligible to participate must also limit outside school activities to eight hours per week in any single activity and may not exceed twenty hours per week for all activities. Furthermore, a student may not miss any one class more than ten times for participation in extracurricular activities. South Carolina and West Virginia require high school students to have an average passing grade in their academic work in order to be eligible to participate in inter-scholastic activities.

Primacy of the Classroom

The heart of the learning process is, of course, what transpires in the classroom. The dynamic of teaching — the use of time, the exchange between the student and teacher, the organization and presentation of the curriculum — is crucial to learning. One of Lortie's[33] consistent findings in his study of teachers is the primacy of the classroom in learning and the strongly negative affect of any outside intrusion upon it. Lortie's study emphasizes the great importance that teachers attach to the boundaries which separate the classroom from the rest of the school. Interference from the outside is resented. According to one teacher in the study:

> A good day for me ... is a smooth day. A day when you can close the doors and do nothing but teach. When you don't have to collect picture money or find out how many want pizza for lunch or how many want baked macaroni or how many want to subscribe to a magazine. If you could have a day without those extra duties — that would be a good day.[34]

Yet intrusions upon the classroom are common. Students are often taken out of classes for sports, counseling, rallies, cheerleading, cake sales, and a variety of other reasons. Teachers have become simply one part of the organizational structure of schools; both within the formal and informal power structure of schools, teachers compete with others — guidance counselors, school psychologists, school nurses, work experience coordinators, and student activities directors — for the time and attention of students. Much to the chagrin of teachers, these non-instructional activities often substantially consume classroom time. As one teacher — not an atypical one — reports:

> The student activities director called a meeting of all girls wanting to play powder-puff football for the third hour today. Two hundred girls showed up for the meeting in the auditorium! Half of my class was missing. I had to completely alter my lesson plan for the day for a reason I consider insane.[35]

In an effort to eliminate unnecessary intrusions into the classroom, some states have mandated that students may not be taken from the classroom to participate in non-instructional activities. Texas and South Carolina have also limited to one the number of public announcements — disruptions — that may be made in a day. Delaware's state board of education requires that principals minimize class interruptions.

State efforts to improve the learning environment are particularly noteworthy because student participation in sports or other extracurricular activities, student discipline, and use of instructional time have traditionally been matters left to local decision makers. While issues of teacher preparation, credentialing, tenure, and dismissal have been matters of state interest and, thus, subject to state control, the classroom itself and how it is managed have been in the bailiwick of local school officials. In the past, local efforts aimed at insulating teachers from intrusive state edicts.

Curriculum and Academic Standards

The most intensive state reform efforts have focused on strengthening the curriculum and academic standards, particularly in the high schools. The Commission on Excellence reported that few students in secondary schools take advanced courses requiring academic rigor. Only 31 per cent of high school graduates complete intermediate algebra, only 13 per cent finish French I, and only 6 per cent of students complete calculus. Instead of academically demanding courses, students tended to enroll in general courses such as physical and health education, work experience outside the school, remedial English and mathematics, and personal development courses such as training for adulthood and marriage. The study found that:

> Secondary curricula have been homogenized, diluted, and diffused to the point that they no longer have a central purpose. In effect, we have a cafeteria-style curriculum in which the appetizers and desserts can easily be mistaken for the main courses. Students have migrated from vocational and college preparatory programs to 'general track' courses in large numbers. The proportion of students taking a general program of study has increased from 12 per cent in 1964 to 42 per cent in 1979.[36]

The Commission on Educational Excellence also concluded that academic expectations in the nation's high schools were severely depressed: graduation and college admission requirements were often low, homework was nominal, and 'minimum' competency standards were becoming 'maximum' competency standards.

Other national reports sounded similar themes. The Carnegie Foundation[37] and the Task Force on Education for Economic Growth[38] emphasized the need for greater rigor and higher academic expectations. The reports called for more homework, increased learning opportunities through special institutes and after-school enrichment programs, and a core curriculum of instruction common to schools throughout the nation.

This area of reform is central to state strategies to promote educational excellence. As of February, 1985, forty-three states had raised high school graduation requirements while five other states were considering doing so; thirty-seven states initiated statewide pupil assessment programs; seventeen increased college admission requirements; twenty-five instituted academic recognition programs; and thirty-four created academic enrichment programs.[39] As with other reforms, there is considerable variation in state policies, but most states have adopted one of the following strategies: increased high school graduation requirements; increased college entrance requirements; statewide pupil assessment for promotion and graduation; imposition of core curricula; honors programs for high achieving and gifted students; summer institutes and after-school enrichment courses, particularly in science and mathematics; and magnet schools. Some states have also adopted policies regarding homework. Florida, for example, requires that students in grades 10–12 produce one written assignment each week. One item on California's mandated school performance report is the amount of homework assigned weekly.

In an effort to integrate the various reforms on the local level and to encourage local schools and districts to take a comprehensive approach to reform, some states such as Tennessee and South Carolina require schools to submit school improvement plans. California's School Improvement Program, begun in the 1970s, was intended to be the structural glue that held together a variety of other programs. New York's Board of Regents 'Action Plan to Improve Elementary and Secondary Education Results in New York State' is a mandatory school improvement program which specifies instruction in science, mathematics, and foreign language; fixes instructional requirements for grades 7 and 8; and mandates comprehensive testing of student performance. School districts are further required to develop student conduct and discipline policies, to have annual performance evaluations of teachers and administrators, and to prepare competency assessment reports with trend data on student performance on state mandated tests. Low performing schools will be required to submit a plan for corrective action.

Florida, which led the way in student competency testing in the nation, has enacted the most stringent curriculum reforms. The state increased high school graduation requirements from 18 to 24 units for 1986. Of those units, three each must be in science, mathematics, and social studies, while 4 units must be in English. Students must also take specified numbers of credits in vocational education, fine arts, and physical and health education. Furthermore, students are restricted in the number of remedial and non-core courses that may be counted toward satisfying graduation requirements. In order to graduate, students in grades 9–12 must maintain a 1.5 grade-point average based on a 4.0 scale in academic coursework undertaken. Statewide assessment tests are required for students in grades 3, 5, 7, and 11.

California ended local discretion to establish graduation standards and now requires three years of English, two of mathematics, two of science, three of social science, and one of either fine arts or foreign language. State tests of student achievement in science, history, reading and mathematics and expanded to include grades 8 and 10 in addition to grades 6 and 12. Furthermore, school districts are required to establish promotion and retention policies.

South Carolina, Tennessee, Arkansas and Alabama are among the states that have raised graduation requirements to 22 units, up in the majority of states from 18. Alabama's requirement — four years of English, three of social studies, and two each of math and science — typifies the core graduation requirements that states have adopted. States are not only specifying the number of units required for graduation, but also the courses that must be taken.

In hopes of increasing curriculum standardization and accountability and ensuring periodic assessment of student progress, a number of states require statewide competency tests. Mississippi, for example, tests students in grades 4, 6, 8, and 11 and requires passing the 11th grade level for high school graduation. Virginia requires students to be tested in 4, 8, 11 and to pass a minimum competency test for graduation. Several states — South Carolina, Georgia and Texas among them — prohibit social promotion of students. To reward superior performance for students, California has instituted the optional 'Golden State' achievement test, based on New York's Regents Exams, for high school students who wish to earn honors at graduation.

Some states recognize the diversity of their student population and attempt to provide programs to match those needs. South Carolina, Kentucky, Texas, and California, for example, require remedial or compensatory education programs for those students who need them. It is more common, however, for states to create programs for gifted or talented students, particularly in science and math. Arizona provides state funded scholarships to gifted high school students to attend summer math and science programs. West Virginia has established a Governor's Honor Academy, a four-week summer camp for students gifted in fine arts, humanities, science and mathematics. Other programs are targeted to the needs of handicapped students or students in vocational programs. Simultaneously, states have also made efforts to reduce school drop outs. California, for example, provides a flat grant for $20 per pupil for counseling for all 10th grade students.

Administration and Leadership

The literature on effective schools stresses the singular importance of administrative leadership. Goodlad argues that effective schools are those that are self-directing and consequently have the capacity to innovate and solve the problems; he considers the principal to be central to that effort. In his study of effective schools, Rutter found that

The 'atmosphere' of any particular school will be greatly influenced by the degree to which it functions as a coherent whole, with agreed ways of doing things which are consistent throughout the school and which have the general support of all staff.[40]

Promoting a climate of coherence and consistency is usually associated with leadership.

South Carolina's strategy for strengthening administrative leadership skills is one of the more comprehensive. All prospective principals must be assessed for leadership capabilities by the South Carolina Leadership Academy. Principals are provided salary supplements, defrayed tuition expenses every two years to hone skills. They are also required to participate in at least one seminar every two years and are evaluated annually. The State Board of Education is required to adopt criteria and minimum statewide performance standards for the evaluation of all principals. Any principals whose performance on an evaluation is rated unsatisfactory must complete a training program approved by the State Board of Education's Leadership Academy or the local school district. Principals who continue to perform unsatisfactorily can be demoted. On the other hand, the state will provide financial rewards to principals who demonstrate superior performance or productivity.

Arizona and Louisiana established principals' academies, while California provided $2 million for administrative training centers to improve the leadership skills of administrators. Administrative competence becomes all the more important with enactment of reforms aimed at improving the teaching profession. Teacher evaluation, for purposes of incentive pay, has become a more critical and visible process than the annual or semi-annual evaluation which often is nothing more than a formal exercise. With increasing emphasis on a more critical appraisal of teachers comes the concomitant need for administrators to be competent evaluators. The debate over enactment of California's comprehensive reform measure focused on various issues concerning teacher evaluation, dismissal, and discipline. When performance evaluation promised to be more consequential, teacher groups mistrusted both the competence and the motives of principals to carry out their new responsibilities.

The visibility of the principal as an educational leader is further heightened by state reforms which emphasize school and district level accountability. They do so either by holding administrators directly responsible for pupil performance or through more indirect mechanisms such as school improvement plans, school incentive plans, and the like. Illinois administrators may lose their credentials if they fail to perform satisfactorily. Missouri and Georgia both require school improvement plans as a basis for accreditation and evaluation. Where schools or districts receive cash bonuses for improved pupil performance, administrators are presumably under considerable pressure to produce results.

Academic Bankruptcy

Perhaps the strongest show of state commitment to leadership has been made by those states with 'academic bankruptcy' policies. These give those states authority to intervene and, in some cases, take over administration of local school districts. Four states — Texas, South Carolina, Arkansas, and Kentucky — have incorporated such policies into their reforms. In Kentucky, school districts where students fail to meet state established achievement levels on basic skill tests receive state assistance to improve their performance. State intervention may require districts to reallocate resources to address specific program and service needs. If the district fails to implement the state's plan, the state may limit the district's authority to spend money, hire or fire personnel, or set the school calendar.

The Texas state board of education is charged with establishing new performance based accreditation standards and a new accreditation process. The Texas Education Agency (TEA) is required to investigate each district's compliance with the regulations once every three years and suggest improvement or sources of aid to the board of trustees and campus administrators. TEA is also charged with providing assistance to districts that have difficulty meeting accreditation standards. If a district fails to satisfy the accreditation standards, the Commissioner of Education must apply progressively more severe sanctions, ranging from confidential notice of a deficiency through appointment of a master to run the district. If these sanctions do not produce compliance, the State Board of Education is ordered to revoke the district's accreditation and withhold state funds, in which event appointment of a master is mandatory.

Funding

In the 1960s and 1970s, school finance focused on the equitable allocation of resources. While that dimension remains a component of state school finance reform, there remains a need to fund initiatives to improve educational quality. Paying for reforms such as merit pay, career ladders, teachers and administrator academies, lower pupil-teacher ratios, remedial and compensatory programs, enrichment programs and speical academies, magnet schools, longer school days and extended school calendars, scholarship and loan forgiveness programs, and the rest often requires greater state financial support.

A number of states have increased taxes to pay for these reforms. Iowa enacted a 1 per cent increase in sales tax, and Iowa districts may seek voter approval of local property tax levies to pay for school improvement projects. Oklahoma, South Carolina, Texas, Arkansas, Idaho, Louisiana and Tennessee each enacted a one cent sales tax to fund educational reforms.

It is difficult to place a price tag on the cost of reform, since that would involve the nearly impossible task of disentangling general apportionment funds from those that are used either directly or indirectly for reforms. What is clear, however, is that some states are providing substantial increases to education. Between 1983 and 1986, for instance, California increased state support for K–12 by roughly $3 billion, almost 10 per cent annually and well beyond the rate of inflation.[41] The New York state legislature passed a $462 million increase in state aid to its public schools in April, 1985, bringing to nearly $1 billion the amount that it has invested in elementary and secondary education in two years.[42]

Some states are also seeking non-traditional sources of support for schools. States that have developed partnerships with their business communities are, in some instances, also looking to businesses as sources of support. California, for example, provides income tax credits for the charitable donation of high technology equipment. Idaho also allows income tax credits for charitable gifts to public schools and libraries.

Conclusion

State efforts to reform public education over the past several years have generated myriad strategies directed at complex and often vaguely understood problems. Some of the reforms, such as California's, take the form of incentives to districts. Others, such as those in Texas, overturn and restructure traditional patterns of governance, authority, and accountability. Yet while reform efforts are prolific, little is known about the effects of various strategies that states have adopted or about the problems associated with their implementation.

For those states that have enacted omnibus reform packages, uncertainty and complexity become partners in the process. The organizational characteristics of schools are partly responsible for the uncertainty: the complexity of schools as organizations, the multiplicity of motives that animate the behavior of students and teachers, the unpredictability of incentives and priorities, the absence of clearly defined goals, and wide differences in institutional capacity.[43] School reform efforts in California, for instance, must take into account the response to those reform initiatives of teachers, administrators, parents, students, and trustees in over 1000 school districts, as well as the state department of education, the state board of education, and a large number of education interest groups with competing agendas. That is why implementation is so problematic. Even under the best of conditions, the relationship between policy goals and their implementation is tentative.

Consonance between policy goals and the steps necessary to successfully effect them is the fusion of policy ends and means. At best, it is a difficult union to attain. When policy goals are elusive — as by definition they must be when they seek to define excellence — fashioning rules to implement them appears a contradiction in terms. Duty and responsibility, like grammar, readily lend themselves to codification and rules; while aspirations and excellence, like literature, cannot be reduced to stringent form.

The general goals of education reform, as defined by the Commission on Excellence, have been broadly embraced. That is no surprise. Everyone wants good schools. Everyone wants committed, talented, and energetic teachers. Everyone wants schools that are as good as those of other countries. But how can those ends be achieved? Parents may agree that schools have the right to regulate student behavior and to determine standards and expectations for student performance generally, but they may not agree if their child is prohibited from showing a prize bull, from being a cheerleader, or from playing football because he flunked a class.

Notes and References

1. *New York Times*, 'Education Survey' (Spring, 1985)
2. See Paul Berman and Dan Weiler *Improving Student Performance in Cali-*

fornia (Berkeley, CA: California Business Roundtable. 1983). Also Loren Kaye *Making the Grade? Assessing School District Progress on SB 813* (Sacramento, CA: California Tax Foundation. 1985)

3. National Center for Education Statistics *Bulletin* (US Department of Education, Office of the Assistant Secretary for Educational Research and Development. July 1984)

4. Theodore R. Sizer *Horace's Compromise: The Dilemma of the American High School* (Boston: Houghton Mifflin. 1985)

5. National Commission on Excellence in Education *A Nation at Risk: The Imperative for Education Reform* (US Department of Education. April 1983) page 22.

6. Trish Stoddard, David J. Losk, and Charles Benson 'Some reflections on the honorable profession of teaching', (Berkeley, CA: University of California, Policy Analysis for California Education, School of Education. 1984)

7. Ann Lieberman and Lynne Miller *Teachers, Their World and Their Work: Implications for School Improvement* (Alexandria, VA: Association for Supervision and Curriculum Development. 1984), page 5.

8. Stoddard *et al.*, *op. cit.*

9. *Ibid.*, page 24.

10. Ernest L. Boyer *High School: A Report on Secondary Education in America* (New York: Harper and Row, 1984) pages 154–85.

11. NEA Reporter, *A Closer Look at Teacher Education* (Washington, DC: National Education Association, 1982.

12. Albert Kaufman, General Counsel for the Mexican-American Legal Defense Education Fund, San Antonio, Texas. Telephone interview.

13. See Chapter 4, for a discussion of testing in the case study of Texas.

14. See Chapter 7, for a discussion.

15. *Education Week* (28 May 1986). The overall pass rate in 1986 was 96.7 per cent. Of that group, 98 per cent were Anglo, 94 per cent Hispanic and 81 per cent Black.

16. See Note 4, above.

17. For a discussion of state policy issues regarding performance based pay, see Millbrey McLaughlin's study *State Policy and Teaching Excellence* (Stanford: Institute for the Study of Educational Finance and Governance.)

18. Lynn Cornett and Karen Weeks 'Career ladder plans: Trends and emerging issues — 1985', *Career Ladder Clearinghouse* (Atlanta, GA: Southern Regional Education Board. July 1985)

19. Dennis P. Doyle and Terry W. Hartle, *Excellence in Education: The States Take Charge* (Washington, DC: American Enterprise Institute, 1985)

20. Kaye, *op. cit.*

21. *Education Week* (6 February 1985)

22. *Education Week* (5 June 1985)

23. See Goodlad *op. cit.*; Lieberman and Miller, *op. cit.*; and Dan C. Lortie, *Schoolteacher: A Sociological Study* (Chicago: University of Chicago Press, 1975)

24. Michael Rutter *et al.*, *Fifteen Thousand Hours: Secondary Schools and Their Effects on Children* (Cambridge, Mass: Harvard Press, 1979)

25. See Larry Cuban 'Transforming the frog into a prince: Effective schools research, policy, and practice at the district level', *Harvard Education Review*, 54 (1984); David K. Cohen 'Reforming school politics', *Harvard Education Review*, 48 (1978); Michael Cohen 'Instructional management and social conditions in effective schools', in *School Finance and School Improvement: Linkages in the 1980s*, Allan Odden and L. Dean Webb (Eds) (Washington, DC: American Education Finance Association, 1983); Stewart Purkey and Marshall Smith 'Effective schools — A review', *Elementary School Journal*, 83 (1983) for a review of research on effective schools.
26. Commission on Excellence in Education, *op. cit.*
27. Merry White, 'Japanese education: How do they do it?' *The Public Interest*, 76 (Summer 1974)
28. Task Force on Education for Economic Growth. Quoted in Doyle and Hartle *op. cit.* page 34.
29. Connie Hadley, 'School Calendar,' *ECS Clearinghouse Notes* (Denver, CO: Educaton Commission of the States, July 1984)
30. *Education Week* (27 July 1983)
31. *Education Week* (15 January 1986)
32. *Ibid*
33. Lortie *op. cit.*
34. *Ibid*, page 169.
35. Lieberman and Miller *op. cit.* page 39
36. Commission on Excellence *op. cit.*, page 18.
37. Boyer *op. cit.*
38. *op. cit.*
39. *Education Week* (15 January 1985)
40. Rutter *op. cit.* page 192
41. California State Legislature *Analysis of the Budget Bill: A Report to the Joint Budget Committee, 1984–85* (Sacramento, CA: Office of the Legislative Analyst, 1984)
42. *Education Week* (24 April 1985)
43. Robert A. Kagan *Regulatory Justice: Implementing a Wage-Price Freeze*, (New York: Russell Sage Foundation., 1978)

3 Educational Reform and Institutional Competence

The Dilemma of Regulating for Excellence

The over-regulation and legalization of school administration and of the educational process itself has been a cause for dismay among many educators during the past two decades. State and local education officials regard the often controversial outpourings of judicial rulings and federal statutes as excessive impositions on their authority.[1] That is why it is both interesting and ironic that the wave of school reforms enacted by states with the support of educators in the past three years has multiplied regulations considerably. Since 1983, more rules and regulations about all aspects of education have been generated by the states than in the previous twenty years. Over seven hundred statutes affecting some aspect of the teaching profession alone have been enacted nationally over the last two years.[2] The school reform movement has created a whole new body of rules governing the behavior of teachers, students, and administrators. For students there are rules about participation in sports and other extra-curricular activities; about how much and what kind of homework must be done, and about how many times students may miss school before they fail their courses. Then there are rules about what kinds of courses students must take, how much time should be devoted to each subject each day, and what topics must be covered in each class. For teachers, there are rules about placement on career ladders and eligibility for merit pay. For local school trustees, there are rules requiring their participation in training programs. In some states, the law now prescribes how many times daily announcements may be made over the school inter-com system. If schools are deemed unsatisfactory by state officials, they can even be placed into receivership, with administrators — and presumably trustees — sent packing.

Regulation of schooling is, of course, not a recent phenomenon. Schools have long been subject to a variety of state controls, such as those specifying teacher tenure and certification, collective bargaining, basic curriculum, and number of days taught. But historically such regulations tended to leave a great deal of discretion regarding the governance of schools to local officials.[3] The state reforms to implement excellence tend to be highly prescriptive, leaving few areas of school policy untouched.

While some applaud the new state activism, others regard the centralization that has accompanied many state reforms with concern. In a report by the Committee for Economic Development, for example, the affirmation of local control is treated as central to the reform effort itself.

> Our recommendations are grounded in the belief that reform is most needed where learning takes place — in the individual schools, in the classroom, and in the interaction between teacher and student. As businessmen worldwide have learned, problems can best be solved at the lowest level of operation. While structures are needed, bureaucracies tend to focus on rules and regulations rather than result, thus stifling initiative. Therefore, we believe that school governance should be retained at the local level, and not be supplanted by statewide boards of education or national dictates. However, states should set standards and provide the guidance and support to local schools that are necessary for meeting these standards.[4]

The tension between increased state regulation and the need to maintain local flexibility poses a fundamental dilemma in the effort to implement excellence. It is a problem rooted in the nature of excellence itself. Excellence cannot be coerced or mandated. It is a condition to which schools may aspire. Aspirations to excellence are generally subtle and pervasive qualities: a love of learning, a sense of history, a command of analytical skills, an appreciation of humanistic values and the like.[5] For teachers and administrators, excellence means caring about students; being sympathetic to the needs of students with diverse educational and, often, personal problems; demonstrating a commitment to learning; and a host of other attitudes such as excitement about one's subject matter and a commitment to the domain of the intellect.

Aspirations to excellence cannot be achieved by regulation. Rules simply cannot compel teachers to be more caring toward students, require that administrators be fair and just. Such regulations would clearly be unenforceable and would probably violate due process norms as well.[6] Consequently, regulations focus on the things that can be measured, quantified, and, therefore, enforced. Rules concerning the length of the school day, participating in sports, curriculum, teacher promotion and evaluation, and the like become rough proxies for excellence. The danger is that it becomes very easy to:

> systematically confuse rigor with 'basics', success with test scores, standards with hours spent in the classroom or doing homework. None of that would necessarily be objectionable if it were understood that there is a real difference between kinds of homework, that make-work is self-defeating and that longer classroom exposure to a teacher contemptuous of literature or history or mathematics is worse than no exposure.[7]

The Search for Norms of Excellence

The taxonomy of excellence is necessarily value-laden and subjective. But prevailing approaches to public policy rely on rational, legal — hence, enforceable and observable — norms. This creates a tension between formal and substantive rationality, between rules and the ends they are intended to serve, and between policy ends and means.

The specific question these tensions raise is whether broad policy goals and the specific rules and regulations to achieve them are consonant, whether there is a fit between ends and means. For example, do students learn more if they spend more hours in the classroom? Are teachers who have passed a basic skills test or who have been advanced to a particular rung on a career ladder better teachers than those who have not? Will higher pay encourage teachers to stay in teaching? And does regulating the number of permissible classroom interruptions improved the class environment? Certain conditions are necessary, although insufficient, to educational excellence. Teachers who lack basic skills in reading, writing, and mathematics are unlikely to be superior teachers. Similarly, if students are wandering in and out of the classroom during instruction or if students regularly miss classes each week because of participation in sports, the potential for student achievement is undermined and there is no way to create a climate that fosters interest in learning. But reforms aimed at imposing minimum conditions for learning may bear only scant relationship to the standards of excellence that they purport to establish.

Rhetoric and Reality

Change and the Limits of Policy

Stripped to its essence, the goal of educational reform is to change the behavior of individuals and institutions so they conform to the changes mandated by the excellence agenda. If schools and those who staff them are to blame for the present condition of the nation's educational system, transforming mediocrity into excellence means altering the interaction between student and teacher. If students are inattentive, uninterested, and unmotivated by school, they must be made attentive, interested, and motivated. And if teachers are operating under the well-known institutional ethic of 'just-trying-to-get-by', excellence would demand adoption of a new work ethic consonant with much higher standards. But as psychologists, parole officers, social workers, doctors, and anyone else who works with people eventually finds, behavior is not easily manipulated. Public policy makers, particularly in the helping professions, have been forced to confront the often unhappy truth that when the successful implementation of policy depends upon changing behavior, failure can often be anticipated.[8]

Altering institutional behavior may prove to be even harder than changing individual behavior. American schools are highly durable organizations, which owe much of their durability to their ability to respond to and accommodate almost any change or any demand that has been made of them.[9] School reform movements have occurred about every decade, about as predictably as Halley's comet, without fundamentally altering schools. If accommodation is the practiced and well-learned response to demands for change, why should the latest round of reforms prompt a different response?

Resistance to change and the capacity to absorb all demands are two of the more enduring attributes of The Ordinary Organization[10] and schools are no exception. What is interesting, though, is the issue of when organizational resistance or accommodation is attenuated to the point that policy goals can be realized. Stated more positively, the question is this: Can causes of resistance be identified and incentives to undesirable behavior modified while incentives to desirable behavior are encouraged? The overriding question is whether reform policies yield outcomes consistent with standards of excellence, or instead take on an independent life, disconnected form the policy ends they are intended to serve.[11] Do reforms achieve their intended results by changing individual and institutional behavior, or do reforms simply engender bureaucratization and legalization?

Creating Effective Schools: Reality Therapy in the School Setting

What makes excellence reforms so complex is that excellence is not a fixed set of policies that can be implemented under a variety of circumstances and yield similar results. Educational excellence is a condition that transcends rules, regulations and mandates. Consequently, as a prelude to understanding what promotes consonance and continuity between policy ends and means, we describe some of the pathologies of education reform policies. To that end, we should rephrase our earlier question and ask: under what conditions and circumstances do reform strategies lead to formalistic compliance, paperwork, or legalism? When are rules and regulations instrumental to realize policy ends and when do they displace policy goals, becoming ends in themselves?

The literature on effective schools identifies the organizational attributes of schools that make them effective. Mostly, institutional effectiveness is capture by the term 'ethos', which describes a general condition. Researchers can point to characteristics that are found in effective schools, but they cannot produce a blueprint that shows practitioners how to reproduce those conditions on a large scale.[12] Institutional ethos is the sum of various organizational characteristics, the concept that researchers describe is greater than the sum of its parts.

Excellence is a difficult product for educational policy makers to deliver. High academic standards may frequently require individuals — students, teachers, parents, administrators — to change their attitudes about schooling. One of the underlying assumptions, for example, is that students can be made to appreciate the value of education. That appreciation, it is thought, can be fostered with some clever policy engineering. Longer class periods, more days spent in school each year, enrollment in academic courses, a curriculum emphasizing basics, curtailing students' extracurricular activities — these are generally thought to be ways of redressing mediocrity. What policy-makers overlook is that students go to school for various reasons. Some are there because they want to go on to college and have careers, others because their friends are there. Still others are there because they like art or shop classes or like to participate in extracurricular activities. And then there are those who attend simply because state law requires them to. For high school students in particular, school may be competing with other interests — and losing out. Students like to go out on dates, hang out with friends, buy cars, drive cars, and work on cars: all that takes money. Roughly half of high school students report that they work part-time[13]. For a large number of students, school is simply something to be tolerated.

Another dimension of reform, improving the teaching profession, also relies in good measure on strategies to alter entrenched patterns of behavior that lie beyond the bounds of policy manipulation. Incentive based pay schemes may have marginal effects, competency tests may eliminate the bottom 10 per cent of teachers — those who cannot read, write, or compute — but those strategies cannot turn 'a frog into a prince'.[14] Raising beginning teachers' salaries to $18,000 and raising average annual salaries to $24,000, for example, may encourage highly motivated and intelligent individuals to enter the teaching profession and to stay there. But how well do such salary incentives compete with working conditions in attracting and retaining teachers? Consider the working environment in an urban school where plaster is falling from the ceiling, 'street people' and irate parents roam the halls, a methadone clinic is located just down the street, old *Readers Digests* are the closest and only approximations for textbooks, there is consistently no toilet paper, towels, or soap in the teachers' restrooms, mid-term exams have to be cancelled for lack of paper, and teachers face threats of transfer and layoff throughout the school year.[15] It is just those schools that most need committed and qualified teachers, but they are also the least likely to get them. It is doubtful that incentives to currently employed and prospective teachers could overcome the adverse conditions in many — particularly inner-city — schools.

It is not clear either what state strategy could change the attitude of the kind of teacher who describes his work, students, colleagues and community in the following terms:

> His students were 'lazy' and he 'despised' the community. Parents angered him because they sometimes challenged his interpretations ... More important, the community simply did not value its teachers ... 'I don't get inner satisfaction'. He wanted to be regarded as a professional ... But as long as society refused to do that 'I'm not going to do any more than I have to'. All his incentives were to avoid work. He admitted to no interest in promoting the faculty colleagueship whose absence he deplored ...[16]

Teachers, like students, have competing interests. The teacher quoted above had no intention of leaving teaching, despite his professed dislike for the profession, because he had several lucrative businesses on the side. It is not uncommon to find teachers for whom teaching is secondary to some other job. Higher salaries would in all likelihood make only a marginal difference to those teachers who hold second jobs because they cannot raise a family on a $20,000 annual income. But financial incentives are not likely to overcome a teacher's enmity toward colleagues who are 'stupid', students who are 'lazy', parents who are 'meddlesome', and a community that is 'unappreciative'. It is very doubtful that state policies can overcome negative attitudes; nor can enthusiasm, collegiality, interest in students, and understanding of parental interests and community values be legislated or appropriately compensated.

A wide range of behaviors, attitudes, and incentives lies beyond the purview of state policy.[17] The effects of schooling are mitigated by various factors. As education researchers have found, poor children who come from what are euphemistically called 'disadvantaged homes', who live in slum neighborhoods with all their usual attributes, and who do not encounter role models committed to the work ethic will not usually benefit as much from schooling as a child from an upper-middle class, suburban family. Some schools clearly do a better job teaching poor, inner-city children than other schools. But it is not easy to create educational policy from a handful of success stories. Government lacks resources to change people's life styles, their health habits, and associations. When the Commission on Excellence tells parents that they 'bear a responsibility to participate actively in (the) child's education'; 'that they should encourage more diligent study and discourage satisfaction with mediocrity', it is only being sensible — but who is to enforce sensibility? The commission's report tells parents to monitor their children's study; encourage good study habits; nurture the child's curiosity, creativity, and confidence; and, above all, 'exhibit a commitment to continued learning in your own life'. And finally, it urges parents to 'help your children understand that excellence in education cannot be achieved without intellectual and moral integrity coupled with hard work and commitment. Children will look to their parents and teachers as models of these virtues'.[18]

As normative propositions, these recommendations make sense. But even a casual observer of everyday life knows that translating those propositions into realizable outcomes is beyond the capacities of government. This is not to say that the conditions to which the commission would have all parents aspire do not exist. Indeed they do. There are parents who have long been behaving as the commission says they should. But the evidence points to the fact that these families tend to be wealthy, have high levels of educational attainment, and place a high value on education. Providing the kind of support in the home and community that the commission suggests requires resources, such as time and experience, in quantities unavailable to many people. Not all communities know what it takes to promote excellence in the schools or have the skills and broad community support necessary for its realization. Particularly in poor communities, those kinds of resources tend to be in short supply.

Delivering educational excellence is difficult not only because it partly depends upon government's uncertain ability to change behavior, but also because the organizations responsible for implementing policies lack the resources to do so. Even if schools paid teachers higher salaries, for example, there is a limit to the number of competent people that can be recruited to teach. Schools often have to settle for what they can get. Public attention has been drawn to the fact that the United States may be facing a severe teachers' shortage over the next decade,[19] particularly in mathematics and science.[20] Houston Independent School District, for example, advertised for teachers in shopping malls in order to fill its teaching vacancies.

Educational Excellence and Cultural Values

Educational reform that aspires to excellence must also address the broader issue of education and cultural values. The inseparability of the two, education and cultural values, is suggested by John Adams in a letter to his wife, Abigail:

> Human nature with all its infirmities and deprivations is still capable of great things. It is capable of attaining to degrees of wisdom and goodness which, we have reason to believe, appear respectable in the estimation of superior intelligence. Education makes a greater difference between man and man than between man and brute. The virtues and powers to which men may be trained by early education and constant discipline are truly sublime and astonishing. It should be your care therefore, and mine, to elevate the minds of our children and exalt their courage to accelerate and animate their industry and activity, to excite in them a habitual contempt for meanness,

abhorrence of injustice and inhumanity, and an ambition to excel in every capacity, faculty, and virtue. If we suffer their minds to grovel and creep in infancy, they will grovel all their lives. Their bodies must also be hardened, as well as their souls exalted. Without strength and activity, the vigor of the body and the brightest mental excellence will be eclipsed and obscured.[21]

Educational excellence, and all that Adams attributes to it, implies an interest in education for its intrinsic value, because of its inseparability from individual aspirations. The fact is, however, that since the end of the nineteenth century education has not generally been appreciated for its own intrinsic value but for what it could do — for its instrumental value. At various times over the past eighty years, education has been regarded as creating social and political harmony by integrating immigrants into the mainstream of American life, as creating a more 'efficient' society ordered along industrial forms, as promoting social progressivism, as saving the nation from totalitarian communism, and as helping to regain America's competitive edge in international economic markets.

As long as education is regarded instrumentally, its value in American culture will most likely vary with the social, economic or political necessities of the day. That is why a crisis mentality has pervaded educational policy. In 1957, Sputnik shook the nation's confidence as the Soviet Union threatened to outdistance the United States in scientific discovery and technological development. Soviet Premier Nikita Khrushchev's very public threat — 'We will bury you' — delivered in the United Nations was a clear enough indication that the Soviet threat of domination was meant in earnest. The threat to national security prompted a wave of school reforms. By the mid-1960s, attention was focused inward, on domestic issues, and education was drafted into the war on poverty, as the avenue to social equality. In the 1980s attention turned abroad again, particularly in Japan's direction, as the American economy began to falter in the face of foreign competition. The loss of America's competitive edge to Japan was partly attributed to the associated superiority Japan's educational system.

While it is both understandable and natural that mass education in a democratic society be appreciated for its instrumentality, that is one reason for the nation's sporadic public commitment to education. The latest round of reforms was not promoted on the grounds that education, like virtue, is its own reward, but on the grounds that the reforms would make the nation economically more productive, efficient and responsive. In California, Republican lawmakers believed that they had to justify to their constituents more money for education on grounds of increased productivity. That is why they would not agree to additional funding provisions in the state's massive educational reform legislation until provisions were added to lengthen the school day and school year.

The instrumental view of education is part of a national penchant for pragmatism — for focusing on what works — that is rooted in American culture. But when the crisis that education is to solve disappears, so does the public's interest. Education in America, especially since World War II, has been subject to these episodic waves of public concern followed by periods of neglect.

Public ambivalence over the cultural role of education is another obstacle to excellence. This ambivalence is manifested in the tension between the democratic ideal of equality on the one hand, and excellence on the other. One critic of the schools states that:

> ... the United States has been increasingly bedevilled by a counterfeit egalitarianism that confuses opportunity with performance and demands that all institutions within a democratic society be organized on the basis of one man, one vote and on the debased assumption that because in a democracy each man has a right to his own opinion, each opinion is equally valid.[22]

The tension between egalitarian goals, on the one hand, and excellence on the other has generally been resolved in the schools in favor of a blandness notable for its absence of clear values.[23] Over the past twenty years, aspirations to excellence have carried the taint of 'elitism' and social regressivity. 'Elitism' and 'elitist' have become derogatory terms, to be assiduously avoided, in the lexicon of educators. Excellence requires making value judgments, and fairly strong ones at that. However, organizing institutional life around value judgments based on excellence requires a sense of shared purpose and community uncommon in the public schools.

The Pathologies of Educational Reform

Integrating excellence into the organizational consciousness of schools means transforming institutional and individual incentives, behaviors, and attitudes, as well as cultural values. Policy objectives must be clear; and there must also be a logical connection between policy goals and the standards to effect them. Policy goals must be based upon defensible criteria. Policy makers should anticipate effects of policies. And, organizations must have the capacity to implement policies.[24]

Why should educators regard the current round of reforms differently from what has gone before? For some educators, the reform movement is just one more source of pressure to contend with. As one high school teacher stated 'I've seen a lot of reforms and changes come and go during the twenty-three years that I've been teaching. But teachers always adjust, and nothing ever really changes'.[25] Consequently, instead of reforms changing the system, reforms themselves are recast to meet organizational needs. In those serendipitous situations in which reform goals and organizational needs coincide, policy implementation may be successful. Such a situation, however, obviates any rationale for policy planning, as outcomes are not subject to control by planners but are determined instead by idiosyncratic and parochial factors.

The Search for Attainable Objectives

A common strategy that is available to organizations when objectives cannot be met is to simply change the objectives and substitute objectives that can be attained.

> Because organizations wish to be regarded as successful, they try to replace objectives whose achievement depends on variables either unknown or outside their control with objectives that can be attained by manipulating the instruments that those groups do control.[26]

Rather than transforming reality — changing the conditions that gave rise to reform initially — specific reform policies and strategies are themselves transformed into goals. Policy means become policy ends. They assume a life of their own, independent of the purpose they were intended to serve. Other manifestations of organizational retreat from unattainable objectives include the displacement of external objectives with more internal procedures; and the equalizing or standardizing of outputs, so that outcomes are measured by organizational effort rather than affect on clients. On the simplest level, this means substituting quantity measures for quality.

Reforms aimed at improving student performance offer a good illustration of shifting objectives to fit goals that organizations are capable of achieving. In California, all public school systems are required to submit to the State Department of Education an annual 'Performance Report for California Schools: Indicators of Quality'.[27] The report is based on various measures of student performance, which are compared to state 'targets'. Its intent is to hold districts accountable for student progress toward excellence. According to the report's introduction, the school report will provide evidence of success in meeting the main objectives of school reform: improving the learning atmosphere and improving student performance.[28] 'Quality Indicators' used to measure excellence focus on the types and numbers of courses take in high school; student scores on the California Assessment Program (CAP), the Scholastic Aptitude Test, and the number of students taking and passing the Advanced Placement Test; student dropout rates; and the number of weekly homework and writing assignments completed by students. Additionally, each district is required to report on the number of minutes devoted to particular subjects in elementary school and the number of minutes the district's students spend in school annually. Even if nothing else happens in California, a lot of paper will pass from over 1000 districts to state officials. Some observers have suggested that educators will spend more time reporting various measures of reform than finding ways to make schools more effective.

California's performance indicators represent a happy compromise between state-level policymakers, who need to justify a $3 billion increase in state educational expenditures over three years by demonstrating the success of state reform policies, and local school personnel, who know better than to make promises that they cannot deliver. Schools cannot deliver what they do not control. Since they lack control over the most important factors influencing educational outcomes, they focus on what they can control. This means numbers. Four years after state reform was enacted, state officials will be able to report that in 1982 the high school students spent, on average, 57,728 minutes in school annually and by 1986 that number increased to 64,800. That increase computes to about five or six minutes more per class each day, based on six classes daily, 180 days annually. Other reports indicate how many students take academic courses, and how many weekly homework and written assignments they complete. At the present rate of reform, California will soon be awash in numbers.

Numbers are also important in assessing the success of Tennessee's career ladder program. According to Tennessee Governor Lamar Alexander, that state's career ladder program for teachers is a resounding success.[29] But Alexander has only numbers to define success. His conclusion is based upon the fact that state evaluators recommended more than 600 teachers for advancement up the teaching ladder. In all, 40 per cent of teachers and administrators who applied for the upper levels of the career ladder completed the requirements 'on their first try', and some 400 others 'came so close' that most of them would surely complete the requirements. 'Even that is not all', according to the article.

> Thirty-nine thousand teachers and administrators — 90 per cent of those eligible — earned a step on the Career Ladder in the first year: 15,000 of them took standardized tests, 20,000 of them trained in forty overtime hours of staff development, and the rest submitted to a state approved local evaluation.[30]

These have little significance beyond themselves. One has to assume — for there are no data — that those 15,000 teachers who took a standardized test to advance to the first rung of the career ladder are better teachers for having done so.

One of the principal difficulties with incentive-based pay plans is that they are theoretically weak, for there is no reliable connection between teacher quality and student achievement. Devising defensible and generally acceptable criteria for meritorious teaching has so far eluded policy makers. Consequently, efforts to impose statewide evaluation criteria for what is only vaguely known promise to be problematic at best. What happens instead is that the focus shifts from meritorious teaching to efforts to justify merit increases.

A recent study[31] shows how merit pay becomes a problem of documentation. One school district's guidelines require 'signed statements from (the) departmental chairperson, principal, coordinators, and/or support personnel who are in a position to evaluate (one's) ... performance as a teacher'. 'Being able to type' gave her a real advantage in her application for merit pay, reported one teacher. While another teacher whose application was turned down the several attempts finally received merit pay after he decided to 'play their game ... documenting things that (he) thought were asinine ... and finally turned in a notebook with something like 257 pages'.[32] Teachers seeking merit pay have taken to keeping cameras in their desks, having been instructed that photographs are an acceptable documentation of good teaching.[33] Advice from one teacher to another is entered into the ubiquitous journal as a 'shared professional exchange'. According to one commentator:

> The word 'portfolio' has become part of the educational jargon in many states. These portfolios consist of the mountains of

data teachers accumulate to show how deserving they are of merit pay. Typically requiring forty or more hours of work to assemble, such collections include the snapshots, the journals, the lesson plans designed according to state-approved formats, the names and topics of inservice sessions, and the names of teachers who were given special 'consulting' help. Portfolios also contain descriptions of 'vivids', another new coinage. A 'vivid' occurs when a teacher does something out of the ordinary. One state official who trains merit-pay 'evaluators' suggested that a teacher could be 'vivid' by wearing an unusual hat to class.[34]

Another strategy for shifting from unattainable to attainable objectives is to 'metamorphosise'[35] clients. If policy objectives cannot be achieved with one set of clients, another set may fit policy needs better. This strategy has taken various forms in California. While teaching to the test is a time-honored tradition in the schools, testing for student achievement is a frustrating and vexing enterprise. Students do not always cooperate by attaining the high scores that school officials would like.[36] However, if students cannot be made to get higher test scores, there is nothing to stop schools from testing only those students who show promise of achieving high scores. That is why California's 'Cash for CAPs' program, which provides $15 million annually to districts in which the California Assessment Program (CAP) scores increase for 12th-graders, insist that at least 93 per cent of the school's 12th-graders must take the test. This proviso was added only after state officials discovered that some districts were only testing those students who would be most likely to do well.

In the first year of the CAP program, across-the-board scores for seniors increased, but that increase was accompanied by a record drop in numbers of students eligible to take the test. State officials attributed the high scores to 'the movement to reform and excellence'.[37] A more convincing explanation for increased test scores — one which also explains the disappearance of 15,000 students — is that schools simply redefined who is a 12th-grader for purposes of testing. Generally, students are assigned to grade level chronologically: a students is classified as a freshman in the first year, a sophomore in the second and so on. For purposes of testing, however, schools designated as 12th-graders those students who had accumulated sufficient units to graduate in the current year.[38] By redefining students, districts not only decreased the size of the pool from which to draw students, but effectively eliminated those students who had completed three years of school, but had not completed a sufficient number of units to graduate at the end of four years, in all likelihood the school's lowest achievers.

There are other ways in which problems can be redefined to fit needed policy outcomes. In ranking schools based upon reported performance measures, California takes into account the socio-economic status of the school's students. This SES data is submitted to the state on a report generally completed by teachers or administrators in each school. Much of the data regarding social indicators is left to the judgment of school personnel. The way school ranking works is that schools with low SES indices are ranked with schools that are comparable in terms of pupil performance. Predictably, schools with low SES indicators tend to have lower aggregate CAP scores than high SES schools. Consequently, if a high SES school transforms itself into a low SES school, student performance appears to be much better. Some high SES schools in California have made substantial gains toward excellence simply by metamorphosing themselves into low SES schools.

Organizations may also respond to policy objectives they reject as unachievable or inappropriate through formalistic or 'paper' compliance. In Texas, for example, local compliance with the state's 'no pass, no play' rule — a rule that prohibits students who fail one or more courses in a six-week grading period from eligibility in extra-curricular activities for a minimum of six-weeks — has proved to be problematic. Because of considerable local pressure to produce winning high school teams, coaches pressured teachers to change the grades of ineligible athletes.[39] Another example of policy evasion is found in California, where the $40 per pupil incentive to extend the school day met with resistance by teachers unwilling to work extra hours without extra pay. Consequently, some schools simply increased the time between classes as a means of lengthening the school day. In New Jersey, efforts to implement a career ladder pilot program met with considerable unhappiness. Because of opposition by the National Education Association's state affiliate, only two districts applied to participate. One of those districts was asked to withdraw, but refused, after a series of articles appeared in a local newspaper alleging that nearly all the teachers selected to receive merit pay were members of the American Federation of Teachers affiliate.

Discontinuity between Ends and Means

Some policy goals cannot be attained because policy makers have incorrectly specified either the policy problems or solutions to them. Incentive based pay serves as the instructive example. The prevailing logic of merit pay and career ladder schemes rests upon the assumption that the potential for higher salaries and professional status will both attract and retain good teachers and act as an incentive for teachers to improve their teaching skills. In both instances, policy-makers believe that dividends are collected through higher student achievement. Incentive pay also has some intuitive appeal to policy-makers because of its apparent simplicity and free market origins. Policy-makers think of merit pay as being causally related to educational excellence. While this logic may be appealing, it is not entirely accurate. Successful merit pay plans have been supported by teachers not because of the incentives in the plan, but because it reflected broad community support for teachers.

> (Teachers) saw the scheme as part of a broader commitment to quality education. Merit pay struck them as an expression of that commitment, and perhaps as a modest reinforcement for it, but *not as a basic cause of quality.* So ... (teachers) ... support merit pay for what many of its fans would regard as the wrong reason: because merit pay rewards reflected community esteem for good teaching, *not because they seemed a strong and particularly effective way to improve teaching.*[40]

Teachers, like students, do not all respond to policy stimuli and some way.[41] Another of the study's findings that is both unsurprising, yet significant for policy-planners, is that money was said to be much less important to teachers than good working conditions.[42] Merit pay may motivate some teachers just as policy-planners intended. But the results are neither predictable nor systematic.

Regulatory policies are regarded as unreasonable if compliance with the regulation does not yield the intended benefits, or if non-compliance produces incremental improvements but only at enormous costs.[43] It can also be argued that educational reforms are inefficient if they do not yield intended benefits or if improvements are marginal but create considerable costs. Merit pay plans, are expensive to implement. California spent $44.5 million in fiscal year 1986, Tennessee will spend $122 million in fiscal year 1987, and Florida is spending $10 million in 1985–86 and an additional $6.6 million in fiscal year 1986. While there are teachers for whom merit pay acts as a real incentive, there are also some for whom it does not. It is conceivable that teachers might have preferred to have the money spent for smaller class sizes ; some high school English teachers might have preferred to teach fewer classes to have more time to spend on student compositions; and other teachers may have valued new science equipment, books, materials, or facilities. Consequently, states are spending large sums of money on reform initiatives that produce uncertain results.

Unintended Results

Policy solutions to complex problems dwarf the problems they were intended to solve.[44] The very size and complexity of the educational sector, its relationship and interdependence with other policy sectors, the multiplicity of motives that animate organizational and individual behavior, and competing incentives and priorities make it difficult to predict outcomes precisely. Consequently, efforts to ameliorate one problem may create new ones or exacerbate existing ones. The result is that policies often work at cross purposes to one another.

The school reform initiative enacted by the Texas legislature in 1984 requires that class size in the primary grades be limited to twenty-two students. The particular provision also specifies that this is to be an absolute limit until the last twelve weeks of the school year. Thus, if there are two first-grade classes in a school with twenty-two students each, and a new first-grader enrolls any time before the final twelve weeks of the school year, the school is presumably required to hire an additional teacher for that student.

Another provision of the Texas reform package distributes state funds for teacher salaries on the basis of the number of pupils in average daily attendance, rather than on the number of teachers to which a school is entitled. In our example, then, state funds would generally pay for only 1/22 of the teacher's salary to teach the one additional pupil, the balance must be paid locally.[45] The mandatory limitation on class size also fails to take into account the fact that more teachers will need to be hired to teach the smaller classes at a time that the state is experiencing a teacher shortage and that more classroom facilities will be needed at an estimated cost of perhaps $100 million. To find enough teachers, districts are hiring teachers who lack regular credential, a practice that works against other provisions of HB 72 that stiffen credentialing and certification requirements.

Conflicting policy goals are evident in other areas. The prohibition against social promotion in some states is anchored in the conviction that students should not be passed on to the next grade unless they demonstrate mastery of grade-level skills. But what is a school to do with a roomful of 16-year-olds who cannot seem to pass beyond the 8th grade? When the Philadelphia school system decided to abandon its practice of social promotion of students in grades one through eight in favor of merit promotion, school officials quickly learned that the new policy would cause some problems. District staff found that nearly 40 per cent of students would be unable to meet promotion standards that would have required them to read, write and compute at grade level. When district officials discovered that they lacked the money to provide remedial education to roughly 40,000 students whose academic performance was below grade level, the new policy was quickly abandoned.[46] School officials in New York City experienced similar difficulties when the district attempted to establish 'promotional gates' at grades 4 and 7.[47]

The emphasis on testing and 'basic' education that accompanies excellence reforms may also undermine quality. Schools may focus their attention to making the numbers look good, rather than developing broad goals that are more consonant with excellence. Districts will be tempted to narrow the curriculum and teaching objectives to those that are measured and rewarded in the state capital.[48] Getting high scores on standardized tests displaces goals that are perhaps more difficult to measure and, therefore, less appealing to politicians, but certainly more consistent with high expectations.

Many educators fear that one unintended result of reform will be to increase the drop-out rate among students. No one seems to know quite what to do with the large numbers of students who already leave school without graduating. The national drop-out rate is about 20 per cent. In California, the dropout rate is estimated to be close to 30 per cent and higher among ethnic minorities. Reducing the drop-out rate is an explicit policy goal in a number of states, California among them. Yet no one knows what the effect on the dropout rate will be of increasing the number of academically rigorous courses that students must take to graduate.

The sheer magnitude of the reform effort in some states creates inevitable tensions among policies. Conflict may be attributed to various causes: reforms may strain state-local governance relationships; reforms may create tensions between state and local norms; or reforms may cause tension between the goals of excellence and past reforms.

The tension between excellence and equity is well illustrated by efforts in states to implement major changes in the standards that govern the teaching profession. State mandated incentive based pay schemes such as career ladder, merit pay, or master teacher programs are vulnerable to legal challenge on various grounds. The basis for selection may be the focus of challenge: what are the criteria for bonus pay? What are the standards for evaluation for receiving additional pay? In Florida, the state affiliates of both the National Education Association and the American Federation of Teachers have sued the state's Associate Master Teacher Program (merit pay) as well as the School District Quality Instruction Incentives Program (merit schools). The merit pay program pays teachers who qualify an additional $3000 per year bonuses. The merit schools program gives money to schools in which students excel on certain tests and other standards developed under the plan. The suit charges that the merit pay program cannot be implemented in a nondiscriminatory fashion because of inequities in the law and the way applications are processed by the state department of education. The teachers' lawyers argue that denying special education teachers, art teachers, teachers of several foreign languages, and counselors opportunity to qualify as 'meritorious' is discriminatory.

Suit was almost filed when the Florida Education Department rejected the applications of those teacher who forgot to use zip codes, failed to use social security numbers on their applications, or committed other, similarly minor, infractions. Nearly 3500 applications were rejected for failure to comply with the language of the rule implementing the program which required a 'complete application'. If one of fourteen items on the application form was not completed, the application was rejected. The issue was resolved when faced with thousands of administrative hearings and possible court appeals, the State Board of Education instructed the Department of Education to give the rejected applicants another chance.

State policy-makers in Florida decided to avoid prolonged litigation and conflict over merit pay by abolishing the program at the end of the 1986 school year. In its place, Florida lawmakers have promised teachers a career ladder program.

Current efforts to reform the teaching profession are often regarded by unions as efforts to undermine hard-fought employment rights for teachers. The Florida teachers' union challenged the merit schools and merit pay plan on that the merit pay plan abridges the right to collective bargaining. The suit alleged that the merit pay plan abridged that right by making the contract between the teachers' union and the school board subject to scrutiny by the state department of education, thereby giving the state unlawful veto power over local contracts. The union argued that the merit pay plan violated the separation of powers between branches of government. It also insisted that the merit pay plan usurped the constitutional authority of school boards by the department of education, since department of education is empowered to alter merit pay plans that have been approved by local school boards.

The fact that there is no stable, quantifiable relationship between teacher quality and student achievement, and no legally defensible criteria for meritorious teaching makes litigation more likely. That is why the rationality and validity of standards for merit pay are subject to challenge. While Florida required a score in the upper quartile of a subject matter test (or a master's degree if no test is available) and one classroom observation as a qualifying condition for merit pay, there is no demonstrable connection between those requirements and teaching quality.

So far, evidence indicates that questions regarding eligibility for incentive pay are more likely to be based on legally defensible standards than standards of excellence. A substantial body of case law specifying teachers' rights has developed over the past 20 years. Substantive entitlement and due process protections are entrenched and unlikely to be easily dislodged. Professional norms based upon legal rights are attractive because of the protection they offer teachers against administrative caprice.

The conflict between excellence reforms and equity is also manifested in the testing of teachers and prospective teachers. A federal judge temporarily barred Texas from excluding students from teacher education programs solely on the basis of their failure to pass the state's pre-professional skills test.[49] The US District Court for the Eastern District of Texas concluded that the evidence 'strongly suggested' the state intended to discriminate in adopting the pre-professional skills test and that plaintiffs' claims that their 14th Amendment rights had been violated were likely to succeed. While the temporary injunction against the test has been overturned by the Fifth Circuit Court, the merits of the issue will be litigated in the federal trial court.

The pre-professional skills test was first given in Texas in the spring of 1984 with the intention of screening unqualified candidates out of teacher training programs. Since then, approximately 6000 students have failed to pass the test, including 78 per cent of blacks, 66 per cent of Hispanics, and 27 per cent of Anglos.[50] In his opinion, Judge William Wayne Justice cited the 'seeming indifference' shown by the state toward the adverse impact of the test on minorities, the 'lack of any coordinated attempt to institute an organized program of remediation targeted at helping students to pass the test'.[51]

Excellence reforms have led to conflict over standards of student participation in extra-curricular activities. The most intense battle over a student's right to participate in such activities has been in Texas. The comprehensive education reform initiative enacted by the Texas Legislature in 1984 requires students to maintain a seventy average in all courses undertaken during a six-week grading period to be eligible to participate in any extra-curricular activities during the following six weeks. The prohibition on participation by students with low grades includes not only school activities such as football but also school-related activities such as 4-H and Future Farmers. Many students in Texas traditionally raise hogs and other livestock for show where they are sold for stud. Hence, raising and showing hogs and other livestock represents both a strong community tradition and a substantial investment of effort and money. When the Texas statute took effect, a large number of students were suddenly prohibited from showing their livestock. Since livestock could not be shown, students were forced to sell their livestock for slaughter at much lower prices than could be commanded for stud.

This conflict over school reform and student participation in extra-curricular activities had to be resolved in the state's supreme court. As students became ineligible to play due to failing grades, parents of those students hired attorneys to seek injunctions against the schools. By late spring of 1985, the matter had become ensnared in a complex legal tangle.

The legal battle over the baseball playoffs grew out of the suspension of two baseball players in the Aldine school district near Houston because the players failed to meet the academic standard required under the new rules. When the players' parents brought suit against the district, a state district court judge issued a temporary restraining order barring the district from suspending the two players from the team. The two players were allowed to play in the Class A playoff game against another district, West Orange, a game which Aldine won. With that, the mother of a player from the losing team obtained a temporary restraining order preventing the Aldine team from advancing in the playoffs. The judge went a big step further, suspending the entire Class A playoffs with thirty-two teams in contention for the championship.[52]

This court action prompted the Texas state legislature to pass a resolution asking the court not to interfere with the baseball playoffs and to let the 'no pass, no play' rule remain in effect. The sponsor of the measure, Representative Sam Johnson, stated that the Legislature had passed the education measure the year before 'to improve the quality of education in the state's public school system' but that judges in some cases 'have looked only at the local issue and, with considerable local interest and emotion, have not taken the statewide impact into consideration when making their decisions'.[53]

The lesson to be drawn from litigation over reform efforts is that those policies at odds with established norms and values may face legal challenge — despite the difficulty of translating excellence issues into legal terms. Parents may demand excellence in the schools, but they do not want their children kept from playing baseball. Until now, the courts have focused on issues of educational equity. The courts seem willing to intervene to protect individual rights, but what influence they will have on the substance of excellence reforms remains uncertain.

Potential for Reform

In assessing state education reform strategies, it becomes obvious that there is no 'magic bullet' that can destroy mediocrity. Reforms often move from propositions about excellence to specific policies to implement them to educational practices that bear scant relationship to excellence. ('Vivids' — photographs in a scrapbook to justify merit pay increases — are a good example.) And even when policies do achieve their desired effects, it is more often attributable to local factors rather than state design. Under these circumstances, reform tends to be a hit-and-miss proposition. How have excellence motivated reforms changed this pattern? If state efforts have made an impact, where and how is that impact manifested? How has purposeful reform affected the conduct of daily business in the schools?

The impact of reform efforts has focused principally on the process rather than the outcomes of schooling. (Policies that specify not only what kinds or how many courses students may take but also the content of courses should be regarded as process in that they represent intermediate goals. Policies that specify outcomes, on the other hand, would be the equivalent of the English and French, generally European, examinations that are required for a diploma.) No one really knows, for example, where schools in California that qualify for additional funding under the 'cash for CAPs' program are on the scale between mediocrity and excellence since there are many ways to make test scores look good independent of student achievement. Similarly, state incentive pay programs for teachers focus predominantly on the process of selection, not on the relationship between teacher quality and student performance.

No significant structural changes have accompanied the current efforts. Some state departments of education have been reorganized (as in Texas, for example) but, in the main, existing structures remain unaltered. No state, for example, has eliminated local boards of trustees in favor of state administered schools. Instead, there is a strong bent toward bureaucratic centralization with concomitant emphasis on standardization and uniformity.[54] The exception to this is found in states that have enacted so-called 'academic bankruptcy' laws which allow school districts to be taken over by the state under certain conditions. South Carolina's state education department intervened in six school districts in 1985 because they failed to meet specified standards. Reforms regarding curriculum, teacher training, teacher certification, length of class periods, length of the school year, student participation in extra-curricular activities, and student performance are all intended to impose uniform standards on schools.

The absence of formal, organizational changes that underpin the reforms necessitate the creation of a regulatory structure in its stead. As a result, reform is organized around regulation and compliance; and regulation becomes the putative link between state intent and local outcomes. Put another way, regulation is the glue that binds reform to the organizational life of schools. Yet as we have seen, compliance with regulations can be subverted in many ways any for many reasons — some of them justifiable. When reforms are not universally institutionalized and compliance is not automatic, a regulatory structure is superimposed over existing organizational structures. This regulatory super-structure often assumes a life independent of its purpose, rationalized according to bureaucratic norms.

The discontinuity between policy intent and outcome that is frequently observable suggests that disparate policies to achieve educational reform are insufficient to substantially change complex and well-entrenched patterns of institutional and individual behavior. There are no formulas for success that guarantee educational excellence. Schools as organizations and the people in them are affected in their behavior by a host of factors. The nature of those variables and the interplay between universalistic policies and local practices create a dynamic tension that shapes the process of policy implementation.[55]

Since policies that have been enacted by states to promote educational excellence cannot guarantee outcomes, the natural question to ask is whether the context of policy implementation is decisive. In other words, rather than focusing solely on *what* policies are implemented, we should turn our attention to *how* policies are implemented. Are implementation strategies that focus on broad institutional reform more successful in fostering excellence than policies that focus on disparate aspects of the educational system? While there is considerable uniformity among state in selection of specific policy strategies, there are distinct differences in the way that states go about implementing reform policies. The following chapter examines the strategies of three states: Texas, California, and South Carolina.

Notes and References

1. See Robert A. Kagan 'Regulating business, regulating schools: The problem of regulatory unreasonableness', in David L. Kirp and Donald N. Jensen (Eds) *School Days, Rule Days* (London: Falmer Press, 1986).
2. See Milbrey McLaughlin *et al.*, *State Policy and Teaching Excellence*, (Stanford, CA: Institute for Study of Educational Finance and Governance. Forthcoming).
3. Dennis P. Doyle and Terry W. Hartle *Excellence in Education: The States Take Charge* (Washington, DC: American Enterprise Institute, 1985).
4. Committee for Economic Development 'Investing in our children'. Quoted in *Education Week*, (11 September 1985).
5. Peter Schrag 'School reform: The neglected agenda', *Sacramento Bee*, (25 September 1985).
6. Robert A. Kagan 'Regulating business, regulating schools: The problem of regulatory unreasonableness', in David L. Kirp and Donald N. Jensen (Eds) *School Days, Rule Days* (London: Falmer Press, 1986).
7. Schrag *op. cit.*
8. Aaron Wildavsky *Speaking Truth to Power: The Art and Craft of Policy Analysis*, (Boston: Little, Brown and Co., 1979). See also John W. Meyer 'Organizational factors affecting legalization' in David L. Kirp and Donald N. Jensen, (Eds) *School Days, Rule Days*, (London: Falmer Press, 1986); John W. Meyer, Richard Scott, David Strang and Andrew Creighton 'Bureaucratization without centralization: Changes in the organizational system of American public education, 1940–1980', (Stanford, CA: Institute for Research on Educational Finance and Governance, August 1985).
9. Arthur G. Powell, Eleanor Farrar and David K. Cohen *The Shopping Mall High School*, (Boston: Houghton Mifflin, 1985).
10. The term is Wildavsky's, *op. cit.*
11. Kagan *op. cit.*
12. See notes 23 and 24 in chapter 2.
13. N. Lewin-Epstein *Youth Employment During High School: An Analysis of High School and Beyond*, cited in Powell *et al.*, *op. cit.*, page 298.
14. Larry Cuban 'School reform by remote control: SB 813 in California', *Phi Delta Kappan*, (November 1984).

15. Quoted in McLaughlin *et al.*, *op. cit.*
16. Powell *et al.*, *op. cit.*
17. The phenomenon is not limited to education: other public policy sectors encounter similar problems. Consider the difficulty of controlling illegal drug trafficking. Wildavsky notes that 'Because addicts love the stuff and the dope traffic is so lucrative, the incentive for buyers and sellers to get together is far stronger than governmental ability to keep them apart.' Democratic government may make it more difficult to transact business, but cannot seem to devise sufficiently stringent sanctions to stop the transactions. Similarly, the criminal justice system cannot change family structure, mobility patterns, distribution of income, social mores, age cohorts, or whatever it is that affects crime. Although for different reasons, the educational system, no less than the criminal justice system, is constrained by variables over which it has no control.
18. The National Commission on Excellence in Education *op. cit.*, page 35.
19. 'Help wanted: Teachers', *Newsweek*, (9 September 1985).
20. James Guthrie and Ami Zusman *Mathematics and Science Teachers Shortages: What Can California Do?* (Berkeley: Institute of Governmental Studies, University of California, 1982).
21. Quoted by John R. Silber in *Higher Education in the United States*, Japanese-United States Conference on Higher Education, Drew University, Madison, NJ, (7 August 1985).
22. *Ibid.*
23. See 'Origins' in Powell *et al.*, *op. cit.*
24. Robert A. Kagan *Regulatory Justice: Implementing a Wage-Price Freeze*, (New York: Russell Sage Foundation, 1978); See also note 9, chapter 1.
25. Teacher interview, Edgewater Independent School District, San Antonio Texas, May, 1985.
26. Wildavsky, *op. cit.*, page 49; See also Robert K. Merton *Social Theory and Social Structure*, (New York: Free Press, 1957).
27. California State Department of Education *Performance Report for California Schools: Indicators of Quality*, (1985).
28. *Ibid.*, page 1.
29. *The Knoxville News-Sentinel*, (30 June 1985).
30. *The Knoxville News-Sentinel*, (30 June 1985).
31. David K. Cohen and Richard J. Murnane 'The merits of merit pay', *The Public Interest*, 80, (Summer 1985) page 18.
32. *Ibid.*, page 18.
33. Theodore H. Hipple '"Vivids" and portfolios do not a master teacher make', *Education Week*, (19 June 1985).
34. *Ibid.*
35. Wildavsky, *op. cit.*, page 50.
36. Students and school officials may also have conflicting goals over achievement testing. California's program of financially rewarding schools that show increased test scores of high school seniors on the California Assessment Program — dubbed 'cash for CAPS' — is part of the state's reform effort to reward achievement. In one district, students threatened to boycott the test through poor performance unless school officials agreed to spend most of the money for removing speed bumps

from the student parking lot and taking the senior class on a field trip to Santa Cruz. When district officials failed to give in to student demands, the students made good on their threat, costing the district an estimated $70,000.

37. *Cal-Tax News*, (Sacramento, CA: California Tax Foundation, 15 June 1985).
38. *Ibid.*, page 7.
39. *Austin-American Statesman*, (14 May 1985).
40. Cohen and Murnane *op. cit.*, page 18. Emphasis added.
41. See Larry Cuban 'School reform by remote control: SB 813 in California', *Phi Delta Kappan*, (November 1984).
42. *Ibid.*, page 18.
43. Kagan *Regulatory Justice*, page 85 ff.
44. Wildavsky *op. cit.*, page 62
45. William C. Bednar, Jr. 'A survey of the Texas reform package: House Bill 72', *St. Mary's Law Journal* 16 (1985).
46. Thomas Toch 'The dark side of the excellence movement'. *Phi Delta Kappan*, (November 1984).
47. *Ibid.*
48. Cuban *op. cit.*, page 215.
49. *Education Week*, (4 September 1985).
50. *Ibid.*
51. *Ibid*
52. *New York Times*, (23 May 1985).
53. *Ibid.*
54. See John W. Meyer, W. Richard Scott, David Strang and Andrew Creighton 'Bureaucratization without centralization: Changes in the organizational system of American Public Education, 1940–1980'. Project Report No. 85-All. (Stanford: Institute for Research on Education Finance and Governance, School of Education, August 1985).
55. Paul Berman and Milbrey W. McLaughlin *Federal Programs Supporting Educational Change: Vol. VIII*, (Santa Monica, CA: Rand Corp, 1978).

4 Three State Reform Strategies: Texas, California, and South Carolina

Strategies and Aspirations

The strategies that states select to manage both the substance and process of educational reform are central to the outcomes of reform efforts. States have assumed responsibility for educational policy-making but, little is known about the effects of various strategies or the problems associated with their implementation. While policy research has focused on the effects of federal education policies on local practices and the effective schools research has focused on the school as an independent entity, little, if any, research has examined models of state-local relationships and the patterns of influence and support that promote educational excellence on the local level.[1]

Yet states aspire to do just that. They have adopted fundamentally different strategies of reform, with differing state roles in the policy culture in responding to the dilemma of state control versus local autonomy. State policies can be arranged along a continuum of control, with high centralized policies at one extreme and decentralized policies at the other.

How states manage the process of educational reform is the subject of this chapter. To assess the differential effects of state strategies to promote excellence in the schools, we selected three states — Texas, California, and South Carolina — which represent distinct implementation approaches; together they represent the universe of comprehensive reform strategies.

School reform in Texas is characteristic of top-down approach, with policies generally expressed as regulations and mandates. Texas shows a strong faith in the efficacy of specific policies and considerable skepticism in the efficacy of consensual processes. This approach assumes that there are single, best policy solutions to social policy problems and that solution are simply waiting to be discovered.[2] As a means to reform, this strategy relies on top-down mandates, centralized authority and decision-making, and standardization and uniformity in both substance and process. An animating principal of this strategy is a strong mistrust of both local authority and the exercise of local discretion.

South Carolina, on the other hand, exemplifies a bottom-up, consensual implementation strategy. Its distinguishing characteristic is articulation of state policy goals, but with discretionary authority and flexibility in local implementation. This approach to policy implementation aims to integrate state policy goals with local conditions and practices.

California is characteristic of a *laissez-faire* implementation strategy. It is something of a hybrid between Texas and South Carolina: policy formulation is highly centralized but implementation is encouraged through fiscal incentives and programmatic compliance is subject to local discretion. The strategy relies on creation of artifical markets in which implementation of specific policy provisions is bargained.

Texas[3]

The Origins of Reform

In a special 1984 session of the legislature, Texas enacted House Bill 72, one of the most sweeping school reform efforts undertaken in the nation. Just about every aspect of schooling is affected in some way. The state mandates not only what is taught but also when and for how long it is taught. Standards for teacher preparation, credentialing and evaluation have been changed. Local trustees are also affected: they must participate in training programs. The state board of education is also the object of reform: a new, fifteen-member state board of education replaces a twenty-seven-member board. To oversee the state board of education, the legislature created a Legislation Education Board, composed of the Lieutenant Governor, the Speaker of the House, the chairs of the House Public Education, Senate Education, House Appropriations, and Senate Finance committees. This superboard effectively has authority over the Texas Education Agency and the Texas college and university system. Like the Texas chainsaw massacre, educational reform in the Lone Star state may have lacked finesse, but few can mistake its intent, a radical transformation of the state's educational system.

The momentum toward school reform in Texas actually began in 1981 with passage of House Bill 246. The intent of this legislation was to strengthen curriculum in the state's schools by standardizing it. House Bill 246 repealed all existing curriculum mandates which had crept into the curriculum over the preceding decades and required all districts to offer a 'well-balanced curriculum', including twelve curriculum areas: English language arts, foreign languages, mathematics, science, health, physical education, social studies, fine arts, economics (with emphasis on free enterprise), business education, vocational education, and Texas and US history.

The 1982 election of Governor Mark White accelerated school reform in Texas. White was elected with strong support from the state's teachers in exchange for promises to increase state funds for teacher salaries, but a downturn in state revenues made that promise impossible to carry out. As an alternative to increased funding, the legislature created the Select Committee on Public Education (SCOPE). The committee membership included the state's political heavyweights: the Governor, Lieutenant Governor Bill Hobby, and House Speaker Gib Lewis. The committee was chaired by computer entrepreneur H. Ross Perot.

SCOPE was charged with examining the state's financing of public education and making recommendations for its improvement. The recommendations were to be considered in a special legislative session. The issues taken up by SCOPE, however, went far beyond the original question of teacher salaries.[4] Lagging student test scores, a perceived a lack of standards in the schools, and a state board mired in controversy over textbooks spurred SCOPE to expand it focus and targets of reform.

Because the poor condition of education in the state's schools was attributed to their management, replacing the existing state board of education and restructuring the state bureaucracy with a commissioner of education directly responsible to the board became a principal issue of reform. The select committee's intent was to break the perceived stranglehold on the state's system of education by the entrenched education community. In referring to the existing state board, Perot stated that:

> ... this is the group that hasn't allowed a new dictionary to come into our schools for years because they don't like some of the words in the book. This is the group that just embarrassed us nationally and internationally with the Darwin controversy. This is the group that has the authority to keep our

public schools current and yet has allowed our public schools to fall behind. This is the group that on any given day can go out and clean up the school day and balance out the whole system between academics and extracurricular and never had the courage to do it.[5]

The recurring theme of school reform, repeatedly stressed by Perot in his address to the opening of the special session of the legislature, was the equation of public education with an $8.3 billion business.

In any basic management course there are certain things you need to do to run a business. All of these things are missing in the Texas public schools managed at the state level. There are no management goals; there is no management philosophy; there is no management training ... There is no accountability. Now think about that in your business.[6]

As highly successful businessman, Perot's conception of school management, which dominated not only the SCOPE recommendations but also the resulting legislation, is anchored in a textbook view of business management. This view asserts that schools are organizationally similar to business and industry: they are hierarchically structured organizations with a board of directors — the state board of education — at the top and various management units below.[7] Orders flow from top down. And the products of education — student performance — can be changed in the same way that industrial production can be changed, by simply altering the factors of production. Industrial output can be modified by changing the labor force, raw materials, or the production process. Educational outputs can also be changed or modified, according to the industrial model, by changing teachers, students, or the process of education. This concept assumes that these factors are manipulable and that educational excellence is achievable by simply finding the right combination of factors.

Perot's remarks manifest his frustration with a system that, in his view, is badly managed, unaccountable, and intransigent. Moreover, he attributes the conditions of the schools to the absence of a business ethic, the corruption of sound principles of education to the absence of effective management. Perot believed that the educational system in Texas was so entrenched and so resistant to change that nothing short of a major shake-up would catch the public's attention.

These views of education echo past calls for reform. The school reform movement at the end of the last century was motivated by the desire to emulate the industrial sector. Many schoolmen at the time regarded the corporate model of school governance as a way out of backroom political control and the way to 'organize on a modern and rational plan our great and costly system of public schools'.[8] Reformers in the early part of the 20th century wanted to make school administration a science and looked to the literature on business efficiency to adapt to the schools. Administrative progressives envisioned school systems that were run as efficient corporations.

Perot's approach to school reform was to follow this tradition. In arguing the need for early childhood education programs, he stressed the need to take four-year olds 'off the streets' and into the schools. 'We're going to love them. We're going to encourage them. We're going to teach them that they're somebody special before they learn to think so poorly of themselves that they never try.'[9] Reform would also focus on 'recapturing the school day'. The school day was to be used for learning, not activities such as raising money so that 'a little country town can send a ninety-girl drill team to Hawaii while school is in session'.[10] And social promotion — 'the cruelest form of economic segregation that can be played (sic) on a child' — was to be eliminated.

Many of the people who served on SCOPE, particularly Perot, were suspicious of the education community in Texas and were concerned that entrenched education interest groups, fearing any change, would undermine reform efforts. Consequently, education groups, including the state's own education bureaucracy, were excluded from deliberations both in the SCOPE report and its legislative embodiment, House Bill 72. Several observers stated that House Bill 72 moved through the legislative process 'like a steamroller'. No one outside of the committee really knew the substance of the bill, and few hearings were held to discuss its various provisions. Several observers noted that alternatives to SCOPE proposals were rarely discussed or considered. The general counsel for the state department of education was unable to review the legislation until the bill had nearly cleared both houses.

The issue that dominated the reform agenda was elimination of the existing state board of education and its replacement with a new board. SCOPE's success on this politically controversial point signaled a victory over the educational establishment. And the centrality of the state board issue tended to distract attention from the substantive issues of reform. 'Once the matter of the state board was decided, everything else fell into place'.

Things would not have been so simple had it not been for Perot. To make certain that the proposed legislation would be enacted intact, he hired his own lobbyist. As contrary as it may seem to the popular image of Texas politics, the politics of House Bill 72's enactment have been described as 'political hardball', played at a level not seen by many in the legislature.

School reformers in Texas had several objectives. The first was enactment of legislation creating a strong management structure at the top to the state's educational hierarchy. Perot argued that 'if you and I were going to buy a business that was in trouble, the first order of business would be to put in top management that could do the job'.[11] The second objective was to improve the quality of teachers entering the profession through testing. Perot held the existing state board responsible for the fact that 'the dumbest folks in college are studying to be teachers and routinely getting teaching certificates'. The third objective of reform was to 'clean up the school day'. SCOPE concluded, based on its findings, that in the 'worst case only 25 per cent of the school day was spent in learning', while in a 'typical case, 50 per cent' of the time was so spent. Perot cited examples of students who missed thirty-five days of school in order to take chickens to livestock shows, and one student who missed forty-five days showing a sheep. Fourth, vocational programs that were 'dumping grounds for the poor, the disadvantaged and the slow learners' were to be eliminated. According to Perot:

> When I was in school, the real challenge was to get the kids out of the cotton fields and into the class. And the school system was really kind of (an end) run around agriculture. Now, we've come full circle. We've institutionalized cheap child labor and we call it distributive education and we're dumping children and particularly minority children and disadvantaged children out of our schools at noon to cook hamburgers and tacos and sack groceries, and damaging forever their abilities to lead rich, productive, successful lives.[12]

Fifth, teachers needed to be properly prepared and compensated. Increasing salaries, particularly for beginning teachers, became part of the reform agenda. Sixth, elementary education needed to be strengthened and early childhood education programs developed. Finally, school funding had to be equalized among the various districts in the state. Existing disparities based upon relative community wealth were to be eliminated.[13]

Implementing House Bill 72

It is rare to find among Texas's state policy-makers and school officials someone who disagrees with the need for reform. Many agreed that schools had become activity centers where learning was the pretext, not the mission. As courses and activities proliferated to meet various local demands, the quality of education was perceived to decline.

While educators applaud the idea of reform, they are also unanimous in their dissatisfaction over specific policies and the manner of implementation. Generally, educators believe that the reform effort was insensitive to the realities of daily life in the schools. Since adoption of the reform package, local educators have been far more preoccupied with trying to implement the myriad regulations than on improving the quality of education. On the state level, policy-makers are busy trying to decide what the rules mean and how to achieve local compliance. Prior to the implementation of House Bill 72 and House Bill 246, most decisions about teacher pay and evaluation, the daily operations of schools, including student activities, student discipline, and curriculum were made at the local level. The term 'independent' in the name of school districts meant exactly that. The state reform initiatives have effectively shifted authority for rule making to the state board of education. The state board was intended by reformers to be the 'top management' that was going to 'clean up' and run, through state regulation and mandate, over 1000 school districts in the state of Texas.

As comprehensive as the Texas reforms may appear to be, however, they are not accompanied by systemic structural changes — abolition of local school boards or state selection of school administrators, for example — but through sweeping and highly prescriptive regulations. Reformers assumed that new rules would be sufficient to revamp the schools. Structural changes were adopted only at the top: a new state board, a legislative oversight committee, a new commissioner of education who reports to the board, and a state education agency that serves the board. However, the new regulatory structure enveloped the entire state educational system.

An immediate source of local resistance to House Bill 72 was that it went into effect too quickly. The new board of education was not appointed until October, and many regulations — those restricting student participation in extracurricular activities, for example — had to be in place beforehand. School officials were frustrated because the state board was not there to interpret the new legislation; they had to rely on Texas Education Agency staff for direction; predictably, they offered inconsistent counsel. Responses to specific questions tended to vary, depending on who in the agency gave the answer.

The new state board found that it, too, was largely dependent upon state education agency staff for information. The job of the new board was to make the mandates of House Bill 72 workable. To that end, the state board's efforts turned to ameliorating the inflexibility of the statute so that the rules could be more easily be adapted to conditions in over 1000 districts in the state. Attempting to fit one set of rules to 1000 districts and to however many schools in those districts in a state as large and diverse as Texas proved an almost undoable task.

One of the most significant issues addressed in House Bill 72, the improvement of the teaching profession, exemplifies the difficulty of reforming from the outside. Perot's hope was to 'put a great teacher ... in every classroom in Texas and keep them there'.[14] To accomplish that, Perot and the other school reformers believed, required major changes in the quality of education that would be impossible without major changes in the teaching profession. While many teachers applauded the general effort to increase teaching salaries and to improve their professional status, specific policies to that end were greeted with ambivalence by the teaching profession. Some teachers and administrators believed that the overall effect would enhance the quality of teaching. Available evidence indicated, however, that the majority of teachers regarded both the required competency test for all teachers and the career ladder provisions as ineffective at best and an insult at worst. Competent teachers resent policies that treat all teachers as though they were incompetent. They also resent the fact that they were excluded from deliberations on policies that were intended for their benefit.

Teachers in Austin, who had won prior recognition as outstanding teachers, were strongly opposed to the career ladder. Their opposition was based primarily on what was perceived as the divisiveness of the program. The teachers stressed their belief that successful schools depended upon a number of factors: community, common purpose, collegiality, and cooperation. Since only one-third of the teachers in the school district were eligible for placement on the career ladder due to a shortage of funds to place all those teachers who were eligible, relationships among teachers had become competitive and uncooperative. They also argued that at issue was not the additional $1500 per year that teachers would earn, but the recognition they would receive as superior teachers. Because career ladder status had become competitive, teachers were fearful that by helping one another they might actually be hurting their own chances for career ladder placement. Finally, these teachers objected to the standards of selection for merit pay. They feared that placement on the career ladder would be based on superficial standards, not merit: those who documented everything — not necessarily the best teachers — would be the ones to advance. Teachers who considered themselves highly competent felt demeaned by the necessity of calling attention to activities they considered part of their professional responsibilities.

If school reform efforts further isolate teachers from one another, the effect on educational quality may well be the opposite from that intended. One study of effective school practices has shown that breaking down teacher isolation and cultivating a norm of collegiality can lead to improvements in teaching practices. Frequent communication among teachers about students and pedagogy as well as joint planning efforts tend to solidify the values that nourish school improvement; increased isolation might well have the opposite effect.[15]

Implementation of the career ladder plan for teachers was further complicated by the fact that evaluation standards were eventually to be developed by the state. But due to the abbreviated implementation timetable, districts were required to create their own evaluation measures. Implementation was further complicated by the fact that there was not enough state money to place all eligible teachers: consequently, those districts that could afford to do so paid teachers the full $2000 while other districts paid teachers the minimum $1500. Those districts that had the funds placed all eligible teachers on the career ladder. Elsewhere, only a fraction of eligible teachers could be placed.

Establishing selection criteria for placing teachers on the second rung of the career ladder proved difficult. Once the quantitative selection criteria — college degrees, teaching major and minor, numbers of credits of graduate study of the like — were exhausted, other measures became necessary. In some districts, past evaluations were used. The difficulty there, too, was in quantifying past evaluations to make them legally defensible. Suddenly past evaluations could be subject to strict scrutiny under due process norms as evaluations become the basis for differential treatment of teachers. In the past, the consequences of evaluation tended to the extremes. Evaluators often give teachers either high ratings, as a means of encouragement, or very low ratings, as a prelude to termination. It is rare to find a range of responses on a teacher's evaluation, particularly if the teacher has tenure. Similarly, the occasional negative comment often goes unchallenged by the teacher because evaluations generally have little consequence in the working life of a teacher. Now, suddenly, small differences in ratings can determine a teacher's career ladder placement. Because of the substantive benefits that attend placement, a high standard of evaluation becomes necessary.

A potential source of conflict regarding career level placement flows from the mixture of state and local standards used to implement the career ladder program. House Bill 72 establishes criteria for placement on the career ladder, but allows local standards, driven ultimately by a district's capacity to fund the program, to further determine placement. Consequently, there is some confusion about placement of teachers who transfer from one district to another. The law states that:

(a) A teacher is entitled to transfer a career ladder level assignment between district, and a district *may* recognize the appraisal of a district previously employing the teacher in determining career level assignment.

(b) A teacher may waive entitlement to a particular career ladder level assignment when changing employment from one district to another.[16]

Teachers transferring between district with different standards for placement and levels of compensation may find themselves moving up and down on the career ladder independently of their professional competence and qualifications. As an attorney remarked, 'obviously (state policy-makers) did not talk to lawyers who practice employment law before enacting this plan'.

According to the statute, a decision of a district concerning career ladder assignment is final and subject to appeal only if the decision of the district was arbitrary and capricious or made in bad faith. According to one legal expert, this provision probably means that a district decision may be appealed to the Commissioner of Education, but may not be reversed unless the commissioner finds that it was 'arbitrary and capricious or made in bad faith'. House Bill 72 is silent as to which decisions may be appealed and who may appeal them. A decision not to recommend a teacher for a higher ladder assignment would surely be a clear case for appeal. But is a performance rating awarded during the appraisal process a 'decision of the district' that can be appealed? Can the decision of a district be appealed based upon the validity and reliability of the assessment instrument used for assignment and that is administered and graded by the district? Finally, does anyone other than a teacher have standing to appeal?[17]

The appraisal process for teacher placement on the career ladder is unclear both in its intent and implementation. The 'appraisal' is the measure of performance for purposes of assigning and maintaining a teacher's position on the career ladder. The state board of education, upon consulting teachers, is to develop and adopt a statewide appraisal process and performance criteria. The criteria are to be based on 'observable, job-related behavior', which presumably means that they are to measure observable aspects of a teacher's performance on the job.[18] The statute also specifies five performance catagories for teacher appraisal: 'unsatisfactory', 'below expectations', 'satisfactory', 'exceeding expectations', and 'clearly outstanding'. As one commentator points out 'after taking such pains to created an objective appraisal process, it is odd that the legislature spoke in term of "expectations", which tend to focus more upon subjective impressions of the teacher's supervisor than objective criteria for measuring performance'.[19]

Finally, House Bill 72 asserts that assignment to a career ladder is neither a property right nor the equivalent of tenure. A teacher who has earned a certificate at a given level has a right to retain that certificate until it expires, is duly suspended, or removed. Whether this disclaimer could withstand legal challenge is debatable. While assignment to a position on the career ladder may not confer substantive entitlement to salary, procedural entitlement to placement is conferred by the fact that the state, acting under cover of law, establishes different criteria for teacher compensation. These criteria, in turn, affect those individuals' earning capacities and professional status.

As noted earlier, there is considerable ambivalence among teachers regarding the career ladder program — a sign of trouble for a program intended to be an incentive to teachers to work harder and to stay in teaching. The point is not that the career ladder program is inherently bad, but that it is hard to implement if it is not embraced by teachers. School reformers need to realize that alienating workers decreases, rather than increases, productivity.

Another aspect of Texas's state imposed reforms that impedes their successful implementation is that the regulations giving them specificity make little or no accommodation for local conditions. The state prohibition against social promotion is illustrative. House Bill 72 prohibits social promotion and declares that students may be promoted only on the basis of academic achievement. Students who have not maintained an average grade of 70 per cent may not advance from one grade to the next, and students may not be given credit for a course for which they have received a grade below seventy. Grades are tied to mastery of basic skills — the essential elements — enumerated in House Bill 246. As a practical matter, social promotion is an organizational response to failing students that recognizes the fact that some students may not master required skills. Consequently, rigid enforcement of this regulation creates serious organizational bottlenecks because schools lack the resources to effectively deal with some students. Retaining students is not a solution to the problem. As one person in Texas asked 'What are the schools going to do with a bunch of 16 year-olds in the eighth grade?'

Since the consequences of strict adherence to the ban on social promotion may be worse than the problems it attempts to solve, the state board of education has ruled that no student may be held back at any grade level more than one time. One study of school reform in Texas found considerable variation among districts in their patterns of social promotion policies. The practice is most prevalent at the elementary level, but less so at the junior high level. The difference in practice is due to various factors, among them the unwillingness of teachers to stigmatize students with failure at that age, and the reluctance to retain older, more physically mature students at that level. Social promotion is generally not as common at the high school level. But in general, districts rarely allow retention in any grade for more than one consecutive year. The prevailing view among the districts studied was that holding back a student for more than one year is detrimental to all parties. Consequently, many districts place a cap on the number of times a student may be held back during the entire school life of a student.[20] Hence, social promotion turns out not to be the corrupting influence that Perot had described, but a necessary response, tempered by the checks and balances of experience, resulting from the absence of alternatives.

House Bill 72 does address the question of what to do with students who persistently fail. The statute states that:

(a) Each school district shall provide tutorial services at the district's schools.
(b) A district may require a student whose grade is lower than seventy on a scale of 100 to attend tutorials in the subject during the following reporting period twice per week or more, as determined by the district.
(c) A district is not required to provide transportation for students attending tutorials.[21]

In this area of reform, too, there is understandable confusion and anxiety in school districts due to the language of the law. First, it is unclear what the law actually requires. Tutorials must be offered, but for whom they are offered is discretionary. Since transportation need not be furnished, the tutorials would have to be offered during school hours, not before or after school or during summer session.

Requiring districts to provide tutorial programs, presumably to failing students, is another example of good intentions getting lost in the process of policy execution. In general, the requirement of tutorials fails to recognize that some students are unmotivated, do not like school, and will not benefit from tutorials. Reasons for student failure are often the result of serious deficiencies that an hour or two of tutoring cannot cure. In all, the permissive nature of the provision, lack of transportation, lack of school resources to provide instructional materials and support, lack of funding support, shortage of personnel and space, and lack of parental support inhibit effective implementation of the requirement. This is why attendance in tutorials has been low.[22]

Efforts to bolster student academic achievement and to eliminate the pervasive practice of social promotion are legitimate and desirable policy objective that are consistent with efforts to promote educational quality. Yet many educators worry about the potential effect those efforts may have on student dropout rates. If students are held back, eventually they become discouraged and are more likely to drop out of school. The answer, of course, is not to continue promoting students who fail to master basic skills, but to develop alternatives. Provisions for additional services are consistent with that objective. Based on existing evidence, however, it is unlikely that district programs created to comply with state intent will be effective without considerable state technical and financial support. In this instance, policy-makers in Texas could have learned from the federal experience.[23] If policy-makers want districts to create programs that deal with the special needs of students, they must provide the resources to do so. School districts do not have discretionary funds available for major, new programs. Even with the best of intentions, schools often lack the resources to respond to new program requirements. When those programs attempt to address problems as complex as continued student failure, the potential for failure multiplies.

For students at the other end of the academic scale House Bill 72 provides the opportunity to take advanced placement examinations, which the state board of education is to develop for each primary school grade level and for secondary school academic subjects. As one observer pointed out 'Although each examination is to "thoroughly test comprehension", the score required for advanced placement is the "90th percentile or above"'.[24] Since percentile scores do not measure comprehension of subject matter but rank a student's performance with that of others taking the test, the legislature's intent is confusing. State board of education regulations attempt clarification by prescribing a minimum score necessary for passing. Yet that is also problematic. One hundred dunces could take the test, answer only 25 per cent of the questions correctly, and if the cut-off score were at 90 per cent, ten of them would still pass the advanced placement test. Similarly, if 100 geniuses took the test, all of whom answered 95 per cent of the questions correctly, still only ten of them would receive advance placement credit.[25]

Top-down policies focusing narrowly on specific policy concerns lead to policy myopia which creates new problems out of old ones and exacerbates existing ones. The requirement for prekindergarten programs in those districts with at least fifteen disadvantaged children is a case in point. For all a program's good intentions, problems with its implementation raise doubts about both its efficacy and its quality. Just as an effective remediation programs require considerable support in terms of skilled teachers, instructional materials, and facilities, the accumulated evidence from twenty years experience with early childhood education programs clearly indicates a need for similar support. Successful programs require teachers who are trained specifically in the methods of the program, careful planning, small groups with highly individualized instruction, and instructional materials that are closely related to instructional objectives.

Compliance with the new prekindergarten rules will be difficult for most districts due to a shortage of classrooms, a problem exacerbated by the limitation on class size that House Bill 72 requires. E1 Paso is building fifty-seven new classrooms to accommodate the approximately 1700 four-year-olds who will qualify for the program. Then, many districts will be unable to find enough teachers for the program. Even though in 1983, Texas changed training requirements for the early childhood teaching credential, diluting one of the critical elements of early childhood education programs, districts still anticipate a shortage. The approximately 1700 preschool specialists who graduate annually in Texas, are insufficient to staff the state's schools. For example, Houston estimates that it will need to hire about half of these 1700 to satisfy state requirements. In addition, the cost of preschool programs is generally higher than regular K-12 programs because of the program's labor intensive nature. Houston, for instance, estimates that its added costs will be approximately $5.2 million annually, not including capital expenses for furniture and facilities.[26] While House Bill 72 allowed $50 million for the program, the legislature appropriated no money for it for the 1984–85 school year. Because the legislature mandated a three hour half-day preschool program instead of a seven hour one, parents, particularly those who work, are either unable or unwilling to provide transportation to their children.

School districts also find it difficult to provide bus transportation to students for half-day programs, for it conflicts with existing transportation schedules developed around full-day school programs. Unless working parents can arrange coordinated child care, their children are essentially precluded from attending preschool. This is not an insignificant number of parents: in Texas, 49 per cent of mothers with chldren under six and 68 per cent of women with children eligible for pre-kindergarten work.[27] Neither school districts nor the state education agency in Texas has much expertise in early childhood education programs. Most information about operating successful programs comes from other states.[28] Hence, the requirement to offer the program is there, but little help or guidance is available to help schools to do it well. Most districts comply with state requirements to implement the preschool program because they have to, not because they want to. Program success under those conditions is highly doubtful. Absent enthusiasm and a commitment to success, programs do not become institutionalized. Failing some commitment, programs, even those beginning with good intentions, falter for lack of support.

The curriculum reform requirements offer another example of the incongruity between the good intentions of reformers and the practicalities of life in the schools. As noted earlier, the two reform bills outline the essential elements that are to be taught in each of twelve subject areas and prescribe the number of minutes each school day that must be devoted to each subject. State regulations also require schools to implement mastery learning models which assume that almost all students can master any subject area, given time and an instructional process that is fitted to students' performance levels. Obviously, mastery learning necessitates a highly individualized learning process.

Three basic requirements of House Bill 246 are teaching for mastery, monitoring student progress, and reteaching those students who have not learned the material. There is, however, a fundamental contradiction in the mastery learning requirement and the lock-step provisions of the essential elements. Some students may need more than the state alloted time to master specific learning skills, while other students may require less. The rigidity of the curriculum requirements are incompatible with individualized instruction, particularly since students must master essential elements to receive course credit. Individual mastery is also incompatible with the requirements for participation in extracurricular activities. Thus, an indirect effect of individualized instruction is to prohibit those students who are slow learners from participating in any extracurricular activities, since they could not master 70 per cent of the curriculum in the time specified.

Monitoring and tracking student mastery of essential elements is an overwhelming task which promises to flood teachers in paper work. Not only must teachers indicate in lesson plans how each essential curriculum element is taught, but they must also document each student's progress toward mastery of each of those elements. Consider, for example, what the requirement means for a second grade teachers. The basic second grade curriculum consists of eight areas: English language arts, other languages, mathematics, science, health, physical education, fine arts, and social studies including Texas and US history. Since the total number of essential elements contained in these curriculum areas is 214, a record must be kept of each student's progress on 214 elements. For a class of twenty-two students in a district where teachers teach eight subject areas, a teacher must track over 4700 bits of information. It is little wonder, then, that teachers feel as though they are becoming clerks, devoting more time to paperwork than to teaching.

It is easy to see how the amount of information that must be accumulated rapidly becomes unmanageable. While a teacher may only keep track of some 4700 pieces of information, the amount of information that must be collected and kept quickly expands as the reporting requirement moves up the data chain. Presumably, schools must maintain records of student mastery of skills in the event that a student transfers to another schools. In any event, schools must keep records of student progress so that can be reported to the district, which then reports the data to the state. The reporting requirement means that 214 bits of information have to be recorded for each student in each grade each year.

Conclusions

If the aim of school reform in Texas was to jar the educational community out of moribund complacency, that goal has been achieved. Texas' educational reform — like everything else in Texas — has been carried out on a grand scale. No aspect of education was unaffected. And there is probably no corner in Texas too remote to know that reform has occurred. But while the long term effects of reform are hard to predict, the short term has been a litany of disappointment. The most immediate effect of reform is considerable confusion regarding implementation. Certainly the number of regulations has multiplied tremendously. Consequently, school people both at the district and the state level are busy sorting through the myriad provisions of House Bill 72 in an effort to interpret its various provisions. There are lots of new rules about teachers, students, curriculum, and programs.

Teachers and administrators in Texas schools that are generally recognized as good (and, hence, in least need of reform) have made the greatest and most conscientious effort to comply with the new regulations. Personnel in those schools have been frustrated by often conflicting and constantly changing rules. In Austin, for example, the administrator hired by the district to implement the career ladder provisions left before the end of one year. On the other hand, those schools that were among the worst that we visited seemed unbothered about most aspects of reform. As a science department chair in one high school stated 'Reforms will not make much of a difference. Those who do a good job will continue to do so. Those who do a poor job will continue in their ways'.

Educators generally believe that the issues addressed by SCOPE and House Bill 72 are significant. And the symbolic value of reform should not be overlooked. In some instances, state reform has actually reinforced local efforts. For example, House Bill 72 certainly legitimized the efforts of teachers and administrators who favored some curbs on student participation in extracurricular activities. The 'no pass, no play' rule which required students to maintain passing grades in all classes in order to participate in sports has made students, coaches and parents more attentive to students' academic needs. The rule also supports the views of those educators who believe that scholarship suffered as sports and extracurricular activities dominated schooling.

School reform in Texas may eventually take hold, and positively affect the quality of education in the state. There is evidence, for example, that in response to the 'no pass, no play', rule, schools have created state mandated tutorial programs for athletes to maintain their eligibility. The importance of sports in Texas high schools offers a strong incentive to develop such programs. Similarly, required testing of teachers and prospective teachers may eventually purge the profession of those who can barely read and write.

Thus far, the most obvious feature of the entire educational reform effort in Texas is its fragmentation. If reform has not accomplished anything else, it has increased the complexity of the educational system, adding literally hundreds of rules and regulations. And while new policies may have shifted formal authority from individual districts to the state, informal structures remain intact. From this perspective, centralized authority simply becomes one more source of pressure to be accommodated at the local level. Since schools in Texas, like schools elsewhere, have mastered the art of accommodation, the successful integration of mandated changes into the institutional life of the schools is uncertain. Skepticism is further justified by the fact that there are often inadequate local resources and little or nothing in the way of state support to effectively implement reforms. Some state requirements drain local resources by requiring that they be spread among more programs. School reform in Texas might take hold if the state provided enough money to fund it.

While it is intuitively obvious that the manner of educational policy implementation is closely related to policy outcomes, in practice that relationship is often ignored. State policy makers in Texas believed that a highly standardized and uniform system of education, governed by a system of rules and regulations that were unvaryingly enforced, would necessarily lead to improved educational quality. But state imposed rules can easily lead to just more regulations that remain little else if schools lack the incentives and organizational capacity to translate them into solid educational improvements.

California

Prior Reform Efforts

Since the early 1960s, reform of schools has appeared regularly on the California legislature's agenda. The nature of reform has varied widely. In 1968 lawmakers eliminated most state curriculum requirements and allowed school districts broad discretion in establishing local standards for promotion and high school graduation. Schools were also given considerable flexibility in the content of course offering. In 1972 in an effort to provide a 'countervailing balance' between local citizens and educators, the legislature established school improvement councils whose membership was drawn from the general public. In order to balance bargaining power between teachers and trustees, the legislature authorized collective bargaining in 1976. During the 1960s and 1980s, programs were created to accommodate the needs of a host of special categories of students, including the handicapped, limited- and non-English speakers, disadvantaged, and the gifted. Other innovations focused on improving teacher training, requiring competency examinations of both students and new teachers, and allowing students who pass a high school proficiency test to leave at the age of 16.

While reform activity is constant, some observers see these initiatives as having only modest and temporary effects on California's educational system. 'As reform enthusiasm wanes', notes an observer 'the measures come under attack. Quickly or slowly they begin to erode, sometimes to the point that nothing remains'.[29] To a great extent, that erosion has been attributable to opposition from organized interest groups. Teachers, administrators, and trustees have rarely agreed on many school related issues beyond the need for more money. School personnel generally regard most reforms as potential threats to autonomy, authority, security.[30] While they have accepted reform on paper, they have fought their implementation.

A 1961 legislative proposal aimed to improve teacher training by requiring teachers to major in academic subject areas instead of education, as current law required. The proposal sought to implement recommendations of national studies produced during the post-Sputnik era which generally found teacher education programs lacking both substance and rigor. At the time, the proposal was a radical one; more importantly, it marked the first time that non-educators had presumed to tell the educational establishment what was good for it. Despite intense opposition from education groups, the bill became law — the first instance, as far as anyone could recollect, that education interest groups failed to defeat a measure they opposed.

It did not take educators long to learn that there are more ways to kill a bill than by a simple vote. Unabated opposition to the law resulted in the increasing dilution of the bill's substantive provisions through subsequent enactments of exceptions and exclusions. After several years, the original law, as passed, had been eviscerated.

A 1971 effort to institute a system of merit pay in the state's schools met a similar fate. Although the legislature created a merit pay plan that allowed school districts to create 'Master Teacher Programs', opposition by the teaching profession to the plan succeeded in stifling it. Because of intense opposition by teachers' organizations, not a single Master Teacher Program was ever implemented in any of the state's 1043 school districts. Several years later, the legislators who authored these measures reminisced about efforts to change schools and 'laughed about the transitory nature of these landmark reforms'.[31]

Another statewide reform effort came in 1972, with legislation mandating school districts and teachers to develop specific instructional objectives. The new law, known as the 'Stull Act', required teacher evaluation to be based on attainment of those objectives. It was a revolutionary plan, for it rated teachers on student outcomes. To implement it, many districts hired specialists to develop district goals and objectives. There were also workshops for teachers on how to develop classroom goals and objectives. Yet after the initial flurry of activity, teacher evaluation changed little. In many districts, setting goals and objectives and evaluation became an exercise in formalism.

Local opposition to state mandated school reforms has been rooted in California's tradition of local autonomy. Until the enactment of Proposition 13 in 1978, approximately 70 per cent of the funding for public schools came from local property taxes, 30 per cent from the state's general fund. Local autonomy was further nurtured by the state's size and diversity, which effectively worked against establishing some central education authority. Localist sentiment is so strong that small rural school districts have fiercely resisted unification, out of fear of losing some of their traditional autonomy to somewhat larger neighboring school districts.

The forces of tradition notwithstanding, external changes, especially during the 1970s, eroded local authority. Proposition 13 and the state supreme court's *Serrano* decision that required state-wide equalization of funding, made school finance a state matter. Despite the state's history of educational reform, there was a growing perception that the quality of the state's educational system was in decline. Precipitously falling student test scores continued to frustrate educational reformers. Perhaps most disappointing to state policy makers was the fact that reforms seemed to have only marginal impact. Whatever decisions policy-makers made, schools in which student achievement was traditionally high continued to do well; while schools in which student achievement was low gave no evidence of improving.

The Genesis of Senate Bill 813

California's latest school reform bill, Senate Bill 813, carries much of the baggage of previous reform efforts by aiming to undo them. It constrains local discretion to determine graduation requirements and curriculum standards. In other instances, it tries to modify prior statutes that protect teachers from dismissal and layoffs. And just as earlier reform efforts could be undermined by opposition from the education establishment, current reforms face similar challenge.

The genesis of Senate Bill 813 is traceable to several sources. The California Business Roundtable, a group of influential business and industry leaders, became increasingly disenchanted with the quality of education in the state's public schools. Just prior to the 1982 electoral campaign for superintendent of public instruction, the group's dissatisfaction with public education reached the point where some members were privately suggesting that perhaps educational vouchers were the only way to improve the quality of the schools. Some argued that since much of the school's poor academic performance was attributable to educators, it was unlikely that reform would generate from within the system. Others expressed the view that unionization of teachers had placed a strangle-hold on the schools and that the professional education organizations were pursuing narrow, parochial interests at the expense of educating children. The Business Roundtable commissioned a study of the state's school system, whose findings affirmed the erosion of educational quality in the state. The prominence of the business group helped focus public attention on the need for educational reform. The report caught the attention of the newly elected governor and members of the legislature.

Bill Honig's successful challenge to three-term incumbent Wilson Riles in the 1982 race for superintendent of public instruction made educational reform a major state issue. He painted a Norman Rockwell picture of education that had been lost to neglect and permissiveness; and he criticized schools for their lax discipline, requiring little or no homework of students, and generally low expectations. While Riles stressed the fact that the problem was lack of money, particularly since passage of Proposition 13, which shifted the burden of financial support for schools predominantly to the state, Honig insisted that the problems in the schools had nothing to do with money.[32] High academic standards and expectations were needed, and those did not need funds.

Since the passage of Proposition 13 in 1978, funding for K-12 education in California declined by 8 per cent in constant dollars. California's per pupil expenditures, which ranked among the top in the nation in 1961, had fallen to thirty-sixth place by 1983. The fact that California had slipped so dramatically troubled some lawmakers, particularly those who were under considerable pressure from education interest groups. However, doing something about declining fiscal support was fraught with political problems. Legislators and their staffs were familiar enough with public opinion polls to know that the public did not have a great deal of confidence in the schools. Awareness of that sentiment, coupled with the generally conservative mood ushered in by Proposition 13, prompted caution among would-be reformers. A number of conservatives who had campaigned on the issue of fiscal conservatism won election to the legislature in the wake of Proposition 13. More disturbing to many incumbent lawmakers, however, was the fact that the longest-serving Democratic senator, known for his strong support of teacher unions, was defeated by a young, virtually unknown, and very conservative Republican. Since no one knew, even five years later, how to interpret the political signals sent by Proposition 13, it was best to do nothing.

California had to confront two politically sensitive issues: how to improve the quality of the state's schools and how to give teachers more money. The solution was a quid pro quo, which traded reforms for money. (Even with that additional funding, the California Teachers Association never did support the reform package.) Consequently, Senate Bill 813 was not only a vehicle for educational reform, but also a means of diffusing competing demands on lawmakers and a way of politically justifying increased school funding to a skeptical public. California schools received an increase in funding of about $3 billion over a three year period, approximately 9 per cent each year, an amount that was large enough to allow lawmakers to mute resistance from teachers. Among the more than eighty changes enacted by the bill are incentives to districts to provide a longer school day and year. The bill reimposes statewide high school graduation requirements that were dropped in 1968, establishes a modified merit pay program for teachers, allows districts to develop local standards to dismiss probationary teachers during their first two years of employment, makes changes in teacher seniority rights, and requires that new teachers take 150 hours of continuing education every five years to maintain their credential.

The Features of Reform

Critics of California's reform legislation have referred to it as 'garbage can in which to toss every bright idea and private bias that noneducators had about school reform'.[33] Educators had very little to say about the substance of the reform bill as it made its way through the legislature. Supporters of the measure — business groups, lawmakers, and academics — see it as critical step to restoring the state's public schools to a level they had attained during a 'golden age' of public schooling. They regarded Honig's election as a mandate for reform.

One of the unique features of Senate Bill 813, and certainly one that distinguishes it from Texas and South Carolina, is that the legislation contains very few specific mandates to local school districts. It urges much and commands little. Most of the bill's provisions are either permissive or provide fiscal incentives to districts to encourage their adoption. For example, the state offers substantial funds to motivate districts to lengthen the school day and year, participate in the Mentor Teacher Program, and hire tenth-grade counselors. There are two chief reasons for this approach. The state constitution requires that all state mandates upon local government be paid for by the state: the state cannot require the schools to incur costs that it will not reimburse. The state's teacher unions also wield considerable power in the state legislature and can block legislation that they oppose. The compromise that developed regarding specific reform measures was to allow the provisions to be negotiated as part of collective bargaining agreements. Thus, what appeared to be lost by the unions at the state level could be won at the local level as local bargaining units could gradually undo state reforms. The changes achieved in SB 813 could thus be nullified locally.

Districts have considerable discretion in implementing the reforms and, as with previous reform measures, there will be considerable variation in results. The lobbyist for the California School Boards Association states that 'some districts are going to do fantastic things with these reforms, and others are going to do nothing with them. You can find anything you're looking for in 1043 school districts in the state'.[34] Such sentiments are not particularly encouraging to reformers. They may cloud Honig's optimism when he states that 'The stage is set for an unprecedented educational renaissance in California'.[35]

The greatest cause of variation in the implementation of Senate Bill 813 is collective bargaining. Since 1976, school district employers and certificated and classified employees have been required to negotiate 'matters relating wages, hours of employment, and other terms and conditions of employment'. In a study of the reform bill's implementation, the California Tax Foundation found that 'collective bargaining is a key variable in determining how well districts have followed through with SB 813'.[36] The critical feature of California's collective bargaining law is what is defined as the 'scope of bargaining'. What is negotiable under 'matters relating to other terms and conditions of employment' has been defined quite inclusively by the

Public Employment Relations Board. Items are negotiable if they are reasonably and logically related to wages, hours, or specific conditions of employment, a category that includes such matters as class size, health benefits, and teacher evaluation. Items are also negotiable if the topic is likely to cause conflict between management and employees, which could be resolved by the mediating effects of bargaining. Finally, an item is subject to bargaining unless it significantly abridges a district's managerial prerogatives.

It is the mediating effect of collective bargaining that differentiates California's implementation of education reforms from those passed in Texas and South Carolina. When the 1983 legislation passed, there was no consensus in California on the process of reform, and a number of specific reform proposals were highly controversial. The mentor teacher program, district flexibility in personnel matters such as an easing of layoff and seniority provisions, simplified dismissal procedures against probationary and tenured teachers, and the like were vigorously opposed by teacher groups even as they were strongly urged by some lawmakers and non-educators.

In eschewing mandates, opting instead for incentives and permissive legislation, California chose an approach between the consensual reform politics of South Carolina and the inflexible top-down reform politics of Texas. It is not unreasonable to expect that a fair amount of uncertainty and dislocation will attend comprehensive reform efforts. Those differences, however, are mitigated in South Carolina by the consensual politics of the reform process and in California by the mediating effects of collective bargaining on permissive or voluntary reform policies.

One of the more controversial provisions of SB 813 is the Mentor Teacher Program, which gives stipends to exemplary teachers. The California Teachers Association opposed the provision because it viewed it as a merit pay plan. Others questioned the measure's substantive provisions, such as the requirement that teachers designated as mentors spend at least 60 per cent of their time teaching while carrying out other duties. The intent of the provision is to keep exemplary teachers in the profession. It provides funds to school districts to establish programs which provide 5 per cent of the teachers in a district annual stipends of $4000 in return for performing additional duties. In order to qualify for participation in this program, a teacher must have substantial recent classroom instruction experience and have demonstrated exemplary teaching ability.

Senate Bill 813 specifies that while the primary duty of a mentor teacher is to provide assistance and guidance to new teachers, mentors may also help more experienced teachers. Mentor teachers may also provide staff development and develop special curricula. Mentors must spend at least 60 per cent of their time in direct instruction of pupils; and they cannot be used to evaluate other teachers.

Initial reactions by local school personnel to the mentor program were mixed. Local school administrators viewed the program as being highly politicized and, so, were reluctant to embrace it. In addition, many local educators mistrusted anything the legislature might propose. Past experience with promised cost-of-living increases that never materialized and fears of the legislature assuming the role of a super school board prompted suspicion. Despite initial concerns, the state department of education reports that in the program's first year, 1983–84, 64 per cent of the state's districts (662 out of 1030) elected to participate. In 1984–85, the percent of districts participating rose to 72.[37] A recent study found that district administrators who oversee mentor programs have grown more favorable toward the program since its enactment.[38]

The initial stages of program implementation required that districts resolve some of the program's problematic issues. The legislation simply specified that the decision to participate rested in the hands of a district's governing board, that the amount of stipend for each mentor teacher was $4000, and that the majority of the selection committee must be teachers.[39] Legislators left a variety of issues, significant for their number and potential volatility, to be resolved by districts. These included composition and procedures for the selection committee, duties and responsibilities, method of payment, use of support funds, and a host of other items that related even tangentially to working conditions. Consequently, the most controversial issues tended to be handled at the bargaining table. A California Tax Foundation study found that even the question of participation became an issue for bargaining. The selection of mentors was made problematic by lack of suitable criteria. As the study points out:

> No strong precedent exists for singling out teachers on the basis of performance; in addition, the teaching profession has yet to wrestle successfully with the definition of valid selection criteria and procedures that, in the eyes of teachers, will be fair, justifiable, and consistent.[40]

The mentor teacher program has assumed very different forms. Districts that had enjoyed good bargaining relationships with teachers were generally able to implement the program without formal negotiations. In districts where bargaining relationships were difficult or where the program might generate conflict, efforts at implementation were abandoned for the sake of 'labor peace'.

Other districts saw no real benefit in the program. According to one district:

> There is great difficulty reconciling the extra remuneration for one person and not for others who (also) provide resource services for fellow staff members. Our governing board turned down the program because they felt that we could lose more than we stood to gain.[41]

Given the ambivalence of many teachers and the opposition of their unions to the program, teachers generally concurred when districts decided not to participate in the mentor program. In some of those districts, teachers were reluctant to take on extra duties even at extra pay. Some teachers were already eligible for extra compensation for curriculum development. In the Vallejo City Unified School District, for instance, a staff development program similar to the mentor teacher program was already in place.

In Los Angeles, the largest district in the state with nearly 14 per cent of California's pupils, the mentor program has been used for purposes entirely unrelated to the legislature's intent. Mentor program funds paid teachers to transfer to undesirable schools. The district had long sought a way to transfer teachers involuntarily as a means of achieving racial balance but had been unsuccessful. The $4000 stipend for mentor teachers apparently provided sufficient inducement.

Local factors generally color a district's implementation of the mentor program. Selecting mentors, for example, presents the same difficulties as selecting teachers for merit pay and career ladder placement. The absence of objectively defensible criteria for selection promotes suspicions of favoritism, elitism and political influence. In spite of the fact that the majority of school districts chose to participate in the mentor program, districts did not seem to have a clear idea how mentors were to fit into the schools' structure. In part, the ambiguity flows from the imprecision of statutory definition and purpose. Are mentors to be regarded as instructional leaders or are they rewarded for meritorious teaching. How districts view the role of mentor certainly shapes mentor behavior. If the goal of the mentor teacher program is to provide an incentive to teachers to stay in teaching, then the mentor program should take on the characteristics of a master teacher program. That is, the program must be structured to provide real professional incentives to individuals. For that to occur, however, schools must be structured so that there is an organizational role for mentors. On the other hand, if the program's purpose is simply to provide a salary bonus for exemplary teachers, no real organizational change is required.

Time and practice may clarify the role of the mentor teacher. Mentors can provide considerable assistance to a school if given a prescribed function in the instructional process and a place in the school's organizational structure. Unless the program becomes an integral part of the school, however, its long-term benefit as an incentive to teachers is doubtful. Much of the program's eventual success in schools will depend on various factors, all of them critical to maintaining the program's integrity. The program must provide an incentive for superior teachers to apply. If teachers become disenchanted with the program and the pool of qualified applicants shrinks and undistinguished teachers are selected, the program's integrity will suffer. Mentors must also be convinced that their activities make a contribution to the school. To act as a true incentive, the program must be regarded by teachers as an opportunity for challenging work, for professional growth, and prestige. And the program's benefits must be visible. The contribution of the mentor to a school's instructional effort and the mentor's effect on student outcomes should be apparent to teachers and administrators.[42] Unless the program demonstrates its effectiveness over time, it is likely to fall into a state of desuetude.

California's unique strategy of relying on local bargaining to implement school reform is illustrated by another area of reform — increased instructional time. While this turned out to be the most costly of all new reform initiatives — $250 million annually in the first three years and $450 million annually thereafter[43] — it may prove to have the least educational impact.

The California schools study commissioned by the California Business Roundtable found that the state's students attended classes for fewer days annually and for fewer minutes daily than their counterparts in other states.[44] The California State Department of Education concluded that

> The average California pupil is offered considerably less instructional time than the average pupil nationally. Overall, typical California high school graduates receive one and one-third fewer years of instructional time than their national counterparts. During the four years of high school specifically, California pupils average approximately two and one-half months less instructional time.[45]

Table 2   Minimum School Year Current Law and SB 813 Targets for 1986–87

Grade	Current Law			SB 813 Minutes Per Year in 1986–87	Change	
	Minutes per Day	Days per Year	Minutes per Year		Amount	Percent
K	180	175	31,500	36,000	4,500	14.3%
1–3	230	175	40,250	50,400	10,150	25.2
4–8	240	175	42,000	54,000	12,000	28.6
9–12	240	175	42,000	64,800	22,800	54.3

Source: Analysis of the Budget Bill 1984–1985, Legislative Analyst, California State Legislature.

Prior to passage of the reform measure, schools were required to offer a minimum of 175 instructional days. Most districts added one or two days to that minimum. The length of the school day, on the other hand, had to be at least 240 minutes. It was up to local school boards to determine a district's instructional day beyond that minimum. Table 2 compares instructional times based on what was required prior to Senate Bill 813, what districts offered, and targets offered by Senate Bill 813.

The study by the California Business Roundtable corroborated what many educators already knew: over the past decade instructional time in many districts was steadily dropping. Collective bargaining pressures to increase teacher wages and the fiscal retrenchment mandated by Proposition 13 shrank program offerings, most notably in the high schools. One way of responding to declining fiscal support was to reduce the number of classes that students were allowed to take each semester. Instead of taking seven classes, for example, students were allowed to enroll in only five. Other pressures to limit instructional time came as teachers demanded preparation periods and fewer classes.

Senate Bill 813 increased the amount of instructional time. The measure does not mandate a minimum number of instructional days per year or minutes per day, but offers fiscal incentives to districts to meet a state target. Specifically, districts which increased their instructional year in 1984–85 to 180 days received $35 per student; districts already at 180 days also received the per pupil bonus. If a district receives funding for increasing the school year year, it may not later reduce its total instructional time. To encourage schools to lengthen the school day, districts were given a bonus of $20 per student at the elementary level and $40 per student at the high school level. The additional funding was to be available in each of three fiscal years, beginning in 1984–85. Districts would lose the incentive bonus if they subsequently decreased total instructional time below their 1982–83 levels. In return for the funding, participating districts agree to increase instructional time proportionately over three years until the state target for specified grade levels is met.

There are three ways in which a district is eligible to qualify: by increasing the school year to 180 days, by increasing the total instructional time offered over the course of the year sufficiently to move one-third of the way toward the state target level, or by doing both. If both requirements are met, the district is entitled to $55 per elementary student and $75 per high school student.

The average high school district in the sample would have needed to add only four days to its school year and six minutes per day to qualify for the maximum incentive award of $75 per pupil. The average elementary district would have needed to add only four days to the school year in order to qualify for the $55 per pupil bonus. The average elementary district did not need to increase the instructional day for grades 1–8 because the requirement is satisfied the addition of four days, from 176 to 180. As the program is structured, districts which increase the instructional year nearly satisfy the requirement for increasing the total instructional time; the $20 or $40 per student additional incentive buys very little. California's Legislative Analyst has estimated that Senate Bill 813 will add four days to the school year and several minutes to the instructional day for selected grade levels.[46]

It comes as no surprise that 97 per cent of the state's school districts, accounting for 99.7 per cent of all pupils, chose to participate in the program. Just as predictably, districts studied a year after the program's implementation had made only marginal changes in their instructional time. Most districts phased in the longer instructional time in the first year, rather than over a three year period, as the law allows. Since many districts had to add fewer than ten minutes to the instructional day to satisfy the requirement, most districts saw little point in stretching that over a three year period by adding two or three minutes each year.

Few administrators or teachers believe that the added instructional time will have a noticeable impact on student achievement. The exception is in those high schools where the additional money was used to increased the instructional day from five to six periods. The more common practice was to increase the school year by the minimum required to qualify for additional money. As one teacher said 'We now do in 180 days what we used to do in 176'. A similar sentiment was expressed by a district superintendent 'Now we are able to do in 55 minutes what we used to do in 50'. According to the California Tax Foundation study:

> ... there were virtually no instances of districts using the increased time or money to hire new staff, reduce class size, or develop new or unique programs or approaches ... Some districts designated certain subjects in the elementary grades to benefit from the increased time. Usually, teachers increased by a few minutes the time they spent teaching the same subjects.[47]

Some districts encountered labor problems with their teachers over attempts to lengthen instructional time. Typically, teachers resisted having to work a longer day and a longer year without commensurate compensation. Everyone, including the teachers, wanted the additional money. Consequently, districts found creative ways of satisfying the increased day requirement without actually increasing the school day. In some instances schools lengthened the time between classes. If, for example, one minute were added to each passing time between classes, the school could add 900 minutes, the equivalent of fifteen to twenty class periods a year.[48] Another inventive, if educationally unproductive, way to comply with the law is to extend the length of the homeroom, the administrative periods used for taking attendance, reading announcements, and the like. As long as students are under a teacher's immediate supervision and attendance is taken, this is regarded as instructional time. By simply extending the homeroom period by five minutes each day, a total of 900 minutes could be added in the course of the school year.

Adding a few minutes to the school day is indisputably an insignificant change. The addition of twenty new class periods each year might have a positive effect on students' achievement, but what that is depends entirely on how that time is arranged. If the school year were extended by a significant amount annually, some benefit might reasonably be anticipated. But, if that time simply represents an aggregation of two or even five minutes daily over the course of a year, the benefits are doubtful.

What California got with increased school time was relative labor peace and ease of implementation. Even though in some districts there were threats of strikes over teaching a longer school day, the infusion of state money for salaries was sufficient compensation to teach agreement. What California did not get for its $250 to $400 million annually was uniformly longer instructional time that is logically related to student outcomes — that is, sound educational policy with somewhat predictable results.

Personnel management is another area of reform addressed in Senate Bill 813. Complaints over personnel management policies had been increasing and many of the complaints were aimed at protection against layoff and dismissal enjoyed by California's teachers. Explicit job protection for teachers exceed those of any other of the state's public employees. Trustees and administrators had long argued that those protections undercut their ability to dismiss incompetent teachers or retain the most qualified teachers in the event of forced layoffs. The report of the California Business Roundtable supported those arguments.

Extensive procedural and substantive due process rights for teachers, it was argued, effectively prohibited the dismissal of incompetent teachers. Due process rights extended the length the dismissal process — up to two years — and greatly inflated the cost — well into five figures, and therefore caused administrators to avoid such action against teachers. Furthermore, initiating formal dismissal procedures against teachers was only part of the difficulty. Procedural safeguards on behalf of teachers were so extensive that courts could overturn district decisions on technical grounds, even when the merits of the case were substantial. Consequently, administrators relied on reassignment or resignation to resolve problems of incompetence. School officials also argued that the early notice required for laying off teachers undermined a district's ability to plan; districts were often forced to notify all teachers of the possibility of layoffs, thus exacerbating tensions. Additionally, seniority provisions allowed for no flexibility in determining layoffs. Teacher retention and assignment based upon seniority was generally based on purely technical grounds with no accommodation in law for competence or expertise.

One of the principal problems encountered by reformers has been their inability to agree on a definition of teacher incompetence. No clear standard differentiates incompetent teachers from those who are marginally acceptable.[49] Teacher organizations have generally opposed any relaxation of tenure protections, arguing that most administrators are themselves not competent to evaluate teachers. Union-opposition to changes in personnel management policies was, however, softened by the promise of a massive infusion of new money for the schools. Governor Deukmejian agreed to $450 million more than what he initially proposed on the condition that the personnel management reforms were accepted into Senate Bill 813. The reform measure also required school boards to adopt a policy certifying that principals and other administrators are competent to evaluate teachers, and that too caused concern.

On paper, the reform of personnel management laws eases constraints on the school districts. The new law changes the time required for notice of disciplinary action and loosens procedures for dismissal and layoff. While the policy changes regarding personnel management in Senate Bill 813 appear to give districts considerable flexibility, the California Tax Foundation study of the reforms finds that in the first year of implementation they had little or no effect on school district practices. In many instances the statutory requirements simply codified existing local policies and procedures.

One reason that these reforms may have made little difference is because of the fierce opposition by the California Teachers Association. Soon after passage of Senate Bill 813, the association held a four-day conference to assess its impact. At the conclusion of the conference, Ralph Flynn, the organization's executive director, announced that a 300 to 400 page document had been prepared, outlining potential legislative challenges to the reform bill. He predicted that the personnel provisions contained in the law 'would be in court for some time ... with legislation of this size, it takes two to three years of litigation before the dust settles on the interpretation of the statutes'.[50]

California's superintendent of public instruction, Bill Honig, has been cheerleading for reform and pushing has own Quality Indicators,[51] but educators are less sanguine. University of California education professor James Guthrie suggests that 'It's going to take two or three years just to figure out what's in the bill. And for it to begin solving the problem in the schools is an even longer proposition. It take three to four years to filter its way through the 1043 school districts in the state'.[52] Suffice it to say that the relationship between educational quality and the educational reform provisions contained in Senate Bill 813 is an uncertain one.

Conclusion

Educational reform in California, as in Texas, is measured by a patchwork of programs that aim in the general direction of excellence but may fall short of the mark. California's reform measure did create some new programs, such as the Mentor Teacher Program, and allowed districts to restore class periods, especially in the high schools, that had been eliminated. But it is difficult to point to changes in the structure and organization of schooling that will substantially improve the quality of the state's educational system.

Conceptually, California's reform strategy is appealing. Local districts have the flexibility to implement programs in ways that best suit their needs. The dislocation that occurred in Texas caused by an array of mandates, many of which are contradictory and competing, was avoided in California. Yet, relying upon incentives and local bargaining to implement the bill's provisions, while a politically acceptable reform strategy, yielded only marginal educational benefits.

An impediment to institutional reform in California, as in Texas, is the fragmentation of the reform effort. Reform strategies are defined by disparate programs — increased instructional time, merit pay, personnel management — all of which may be beneficial, but none of which substantially enhance the effectiveness of schools. Basically, the assumptions upon which reform policies are fashioned are essentially correct. Superior teachers should be rewarded, incompetent teachers should not be protected from dismissal by a wall of technicalities, students should spend more time in school and should take more academic subjects, and salaries for teachers should be competitive with other professions. As normative propositions, the eighty or more provisions contained in Senate Bill 813 are defensible. The difficulty is that they do not necessarily produce educational excellence. Despite the successful attainment of specific goals, the broader goal of institutional excellence may not be realized. Each of those reform policies may cultivate one aspect of effective schools without achieving the overall institutional reform needed to make the idea of excellence a reality.

South Carolina

Prior Reform Efforts

The South has a particularly sorry track record in public education. It was the last region of the country to adopt public schooling and the schools that did operate were crippled by the Jim Crow tradition. The region has consistently ranked last in student test scores, teacher salaries and per-pupil expenditures, first in dropout rates and illiteracy.

South Carolina typified the region. By most measures, the state ranked near the bottom of educational achievement. In 1980, slightly more than half of the state's adult population had finished high school, and students' Scholastic Aptitude Tests were lowest in the nation. In 1983, the state ranked forty-fifth in average teacher salaries, thirty-sixth in the ratio of pupils to teachers, forty-eighth in expenditures per pupil, and forty-fifth in expenditures as a percent of per capita income.[53] Moreover, public confidence in the schools was quite low. A survey of public opinion regarding South Carolina's schools found that two-thirds of the state's adults held a negative opinion about them.[54]

South Carolina's schools had gone through spasms of prior reform. Efforts began in 1974 with passage of the Teacher Employment and Dismissal Act, a measure designed to establish uniform standards. The Education Finance Act, enacted by the state's General Assembly in 1977, was intended to correct funding inequities by equalizing educational finance among the state's school districts. Among policy-makers in South Carolina, this measure is regarded as the forerunner of subsequent major reform efforts. The Basic Skills Assessment Act in 1978 mandated state testing for student achievement. And the Educator Improvement Act of 1979 sought to strengthen both entry requirements into teaching and evaluation standards for current teachers.[55]

Reform efforts in the state had many obstacles to overcome. A legacy of racial segregation not easily undone. In some school districts, particularly in the low country, the end of *de jure* segregation prompted an exodus of whites to private schools. Whites tried to keep public tax support low, sending their children to private schools.[56] Moreover, vast differences between the white and black school systems made attempts to unite two racially segregated systems difficult. Consequently, the loss of white majority support in many parts of the state, coupled with the dislocations caused by merging two distinct school systems, vitiated earlier reform efforts. Low teaching salaries also made efforts to recruit better teachers futile. Even if reforms enabled school officials to weed out incompetent teachers, good teachers would fail to be attracted by the pittance they were paid. Similarly, attempts to improve student performance by establishing a state-defined minimum average consisted principally of increased paper-work and reporting requirements. Student achievement testing simply called attention to what most people already knew — that students were doing poorly.

In the early 1980s, however, regional competition for high technology firms and recognition that the region's economic future depends on a skilled work force and good educational system spurred a dramatic school reform movement throughout the South. South

Carolina was a leader in this venture. According to a South Carolina educator 'In the South right now, education reform is kind of like the Holy Grail. All the politicians in the southeast have been chasing the reform movement. There is a recognition in the South now that education and economic development must go hand-in-hand. A lot of governors sense that'.[57]

South Carolina's reform effort began in 1983 with adoption by the state board of education of an educational reform plan entitled 'Move to Quality'. Governor Richard W. Riley proposed to increase state support for education, but his proposal failed to muster necessary legislative support for enactment. Bent on success in the next session of the legislature, Riley and State superintendent Charlie G. Williams created two blue-ribbon committees to assist their efforts. The Business-Education Partnership committee and the Committee on Financing Excellence in Public Education were comprised of sixty-one business, educational, civic and legislative leaders from all parts of the state.

Reform and Consensus

The most significant aspect of reform in South Carolina is that the reform process predominated over adherence to specific policies. According to those who were instrumental in orchestrating reform, the integrity of the process was critical. State policy-makers believed that the business community, whose active support was deemed essential, the education community, and state and civic leaders could not work together successfully in the absence of a commitment to significant and sustained changes in the public school system. Building trust among educators and simultaneously developing the business community's confidence in the state board of education were central. According to Governor Riley's education specialist, Terry Peterson, several conditions had to prevail. Reform had to be generated internally; unless reform occurred within the system, reformers agreed that they would not take hold. Policy-makers also recognized the fact that reform could not be successfully engineered without broad community support. And an integral part of the reform agenda had to include efforts to create public confidence in the capacity of schools to improve, to convince the public that reform was possible and worthy of support.

The reform effort consisted of three stages. The first was the development of a reform agenda. Governor Riley was committed to increasing state revenues for schools by increasing the state sales tax from four to five cents. The *quid pro quo*, improving the quality of education, was a more vague goal, particularly when it came to specifying policies for its achievement. The second stage of reform required crafting regulations and programs necessary to effect reform policies. The third stage entailed technical assistance and monitoring to assure accountability.

Each stage necessitated establishing its own structure.From the outset, policy-makers were aware of the need to develop an effective and highly credible mechanism for accountability before reform could take place. Since trust was the glue that bound the disparate groups together, it was confidence in the outcomes of reform that, in turn, reinforced trust. Given the mutual suspicion with which educators, businessmen and politicians regard one another, establishing a high level of credibility among them was considered critical to the reform effort.

The policy development process itself was animated by a strong desire to develop coordinated support of school reform among various groups in the state and to shape a consensus on reform issues among those groups. An important structural element in the policy development process was a mechanism allowing different groups to resolve conflicts that arose over policies. According to Don Thomas, hired specifically to establish and oversee a division of accountability in the state department of education, 2800 individuals regarded as the most influential people in the state were contacted. Their support was solicited through the two committees, and eventually the committee members developed a proprietary interest in the success of school reform. In addition to the committe structure, a coalition of business leaders, moderate legislators and state education associations was formed to work with the Governor and his cabinet in order to monitor the reform effort and to negotiate agreements when conflict arose.

In September 1983, seven public forums were held around the state to develop education reform goals. Participants included the Governor, the Lieutenant Governor, local legislators, the teacher of the year, and local business and education leaders. The meetings consisted of two parts: remarks by the governor and his party, followed by discussion groups. The discussion groups were open to anyone who wished to attend. Group leaders would divide the forum into small working groups, and each participant was given a packet that listed general reform goals. Participants were asked to develop specific proposals for their attainment. One goal, for example, was 'improve leadership and management in the schools'. Participants were asked to say how the goal could be best achieved. Then they were asked to list ideas, strategies, or changes to improve the quality of education in the catagories of curriculum, teacher preparation, financing, and any other. The responses were then summarized into consensus reports at the local, regional and state level. Forum activities were coordinated at the county level using local PTAs, churches, civic clubs, business groups, and public officials. Statewide over 13,000 people participated in the public forums.

In an effort to build grass roots support, South Carolina businesses raised over $100,000 for radio, television and newspaper advertisements. A well-known political advertising firm was hired to manage a media effort. One television commercial showed a pregnant woman mailing a letter to her legislator and saying that her unborn child's future was too important for her not to do so. Another showed a blue collar worker skipping a bowling match to attend a forum on public education. Governor Riley also traveled the state making speeches. To further encourage broad citizen participation, telephone banks were established with a toll-free telephone 'hot-line' so that people could call in with questions or recommendations regarding reform. A speakers' bureau was created; education, church, business, and civic leaders are estimated to have made collectively over 1000 speeches between October and December of 1983. The governor's office estimates that over 40,000 people were reached during this process.

In addition to building strong public support, it was critical to the reform effort that the various education interest groups not splinter over particular issues. Riley and his staff held regular meetings in the governor's mansion with groups of educators in order to maintain their support on all reform issues and, just as importantly, to ensure consonance on policy issues between the leadership and membership of education organizations. Issues were determined by consensus, not by majority vote. Policies over which consensus could not be reached were excluded. For that reason, inclusion of a career ladder program in the reform package was abandoned. According to Hayes Mizell, a school board member in Columbia and a long-time civil rights activist, all the issues in the reform package that went to the legislature had been carefully negotiated beforehand with the principal interest groups. The only new issue to come up in the legislature was a one cent increase in the sales tax to pay for reforms. Both Mizell and Peterson attribute the consensus to the fact that a negotiating structure had been created that enabled the involvement of diverse groups in the process of policy formulation.

Successful enactment of the reform package also owed much to the fact that there was, in Terry Peterson's words 'something for everybody'. Teachers were given a 16 per cent across-the-board pay raise and statutory guarantees that their salaries would continue to increase with average salaries in the Southeast. For their support, taxpayers and the business community wanted and got an accountability mechanism, including state intervention in school districts that fall below prescribed standards. Students would benefit from better teachers, new programs, and tighter standards that would translate into higher student academic achievement.

Unlike Texas' educational reform package, South Carolina's included a specific funding mechanism. The increase in the state's sales tax from four to five cents is expected to generate over $1.3 billion in revenues for education in its first five years, an amount equal to total state and local expenditures for 1983–84. Thus, schools in the state are not faced with newly mandated programs that are inadequately funded. Rather than diluting resources for existing programs, South Carolina provides substantial, new fiscal support. The required increased in units for high school graduation, for example, came with an allocation of slightly more than $5 million in 1984 to pay for the estimated 250 science and math teachers that would be required. Other increases included $1.8 million for mandated preschool or kindergarten program for 5-year-olds, $3.7 million for gifted and talented students, $7 million for improving vocational education, $60.5 million for remedial instruction, $60 million for teacher salaries and $9.3 million in fringe benefits (these are in addition to 5.7 per cent increases in both areas through the state's General Fund), $1.8 million for augmenting principals' salaries, and $55.7 million in school construction and renovation.

South Carolina's approach to school reform was essentially pragmatic. Building consensus from the bottom through broad participation fostered agreement on the agenda. Inclusion of teachers and administrators in the policy making process not only built confidence within those groups in the process, but also engendered a proprietary interest in its outcome. When the legislature acted, teachers and administrators were in agreement on specific strategies and were knowledgeable about the intent of reform. That support eased the rush of implementation in the schools. Even though school officials had only three or four months in which to put into effect many of the Education Improvement Act's provisions, educators had a fairly clear idea of their roles and responsibilities.

Accompanying increased revenues for the schools are a wide

range of programmatic mandates specified by reform legislation. In the area of standards for graduation and promotion, the Education Improvement Act requires students to pass a basic skills exit examination to receive a high school diploma; high school graduation requirements were also increased; and districts were required to develop promotion policies based upon state board of education minimum standards. Remediation is provided to students who fail to meet the state's minimum basic skills requirement. Concerning attendance and discipline, the new law requires longer school days and year; prohibits promotion of students who are absent more than ten days in a school year without approval of the school board; and districts must develop discipline codes and enforcement policies based upon state minimum standards. In curriculum, the reform act requires districts to provide college preparatory courses, emphasize 'higher-order' problem solving, and place 50 per cent of vocational students in related jobs. The early childhood education part of the legislation requires all 5-year-old children to attend kindergarten and allows 4-year-old children who are developmentally disabled to attend half-day child development programs. For teachers, the reform package contained a significant pay package, as we noted earlier. Additionally, the law specifies formal evaluation, competitive grants, and centers to promote excellence in teaching. Prospective school administrators are to be evaluated by the state department of education for their leadership and management skills and must take part in approved seminars on improving administrative skills and instructional leadership every two years. At the center of the reform effort is the school improvement program. Each school and each district must have school improvement councils which are responsible for approving and submitting improvement plans.

Interviews with teachers, administrators, and local school board members in South Carolina have not revealed much unhappiness or confusion about the intent of the new law and its implementation — a very different story from the one repeated in Texas and California. The short time for implementation, three months, did pose something of a problem. Creating remedial and compensatory education programs in many instances necessitated hiring additional staff and providing facilities for them. Remedial teachers and administrators needed to develop program goals, instructional materials, and curriculum guides quickly. In spite of these constraints, the strain of implementing new programs was mitigated by three factors. First, since the reforms had been anticipated for some time and since most educators were familiar with the specific provisions of the law, school personnel planned for the new requirements and adjusted local practices accordingly. The prevailing attitude among local school administrators was that the state department of education had been cooperative during the period of implementation. Educators, both state and local, were committed to the successful implementation of the Education Improvement Act. Second, local schools and districts had considerable flexibility in implementing state mandated programs. This feature of reform was important to local school personnel. The compensatory and remedial education programs, for example, have few prescriptions regarding specific implementation provisions. State regulations simply define compensatory education and remediation and specify criteria for student participation; the districts determine basic program structures themselves.

While districts have flexibility to implement programs according to their needs, they are held accountable for the programs' results. Schools must also justify implementation decisions in the plans they submit. Districts are free to design programs that are most compatible with existing school structures so that the disruption of creating new programs and adding new staff is minimized. The third, and perhaps most important, factor is that there was sufficient money to pay for the reforms.

The most unequivocal support came from black school administrators and teachers who, as Hayes Mizell stated 'know from personal experience what it means not to educate entire groups of people'. Generally, this group believed that the Education Improvement Act was timely, important, and 'one of the best things that happened to minority students'. Most importantly, the reform act established the same expectations for all students, black and white. And those expectations now carry the imprimatur of the state. According to a principal in an all black high school, the reforms validate and give credibility to positions that before might have been regarded as racially discriminatory. Principals who had been opposed to social promotion or who restricted student participation in extracurricular activities to those with passing grades, for example, were often assailed for such policies, particularly when those policies tended to affect black students more adversely than white students. Now, high standards and expectations are a matter of state policy embodied in law.

The implementation of some reforms have been problematic. The state mandate restricting students with failing grades from participating in athletics was quickly challenged in the courts, and the courts imposed a one-year delay to give students fair notice. The limitation on student absences has created problems in some instances, when administrators have been too rule-minded. Some administrators, for example, interpret the prohibition on classroom interruptions to mean that a student who is 10 minutes late to class must miss the entire period. That kind of inflexibility, according to one superintendent, should never be substituted for common sense.

When asked how the Education Improvement Act had influenced how they viewed their jobs and, in particular, how it affected the way they spend their time, most administrators responded that their preoccupation had shifted significantly toward the classroom. The reform measure strengthens the principal's role as instructional leader since principals are now accountable for developing student performance goals and school improvement plans. To professionalize the principal's job, the statute requires that principals participate in leadership seminars; it offers salary bonuses for those who demonstrate 'superior performance and productivity'. The state provides funds for school districts to establish apprenticeship programs for individuals who 'demonstrate outstanding potential as school administrators'.

Teachers similarly believed that reform had focused attention on the classroom, particularly on improving the effectiveness of instruction. The pervasive attitude among teachers was that the schools' various classroom activities were much more focused and goal-oriented than they had been. Reform was widely regarded among teachers as affirming the primacy of learning. Both teachers and administrators appreciated the shift from prior law, the Defined Minimum Standards, that focused only on test results and other fill-in-the-blanks measures for school performance to current law with its emphasis on planning and goal-setting.

The term accountability is ubiquitous in reform circles, yet its meaning is ambiguous. One way to think of accountability is as a big stick, used to force local schools into compliance with state policies. Another way to think about accountability is as a means of communication about program success or failure. The latter view is aligned with efforts toward institutional improvement through local planning.

South Carolina's educational reform legislation promotes a model of accountability that is based on local planning and information about how well school are doing. The state requires each school district to submit an annual written report and prescribes broad areas that must be addressed in this report. The reform act requires that local school districts establish improvement councils at each school site and specifies their composition — at least two parents, at least two teachers, at least two students, other representatives of the community and persons selected by the principal. Elected members of the council must comprise a two-thirds majority of the total membership. Councils assist in the preparation of annual school improvement reports, as well as assist in monitoring school improvement plans contained in the reports. If councils wish to do so, they may submit a report separately from that submitted by the principal. Each school district board of trustees is required, in turn, to prepare a 'written appraisal of the school improvement report of each school with emphasis on needs, goals, objectives, needed improvements, and plans for the utilization of resources'.[58]

The school improvement report must address various factors that have been identified by the state board of education as indicators of school effectiveness. These are positive school climate, instructional leadership of the principal, the school's emphasis on academics including basic skills, frequent monitoring of student progress and its utilization in curriculum planning, high expectations related to student achievement, and positive home-school relations. The purpose of school improvement reports is to require schools to develop plans that focus on specific goals and objectives. Schools assess their strengths and weaknesses in various areas including student performance, drop-out rates, and community involvement. Ideally, the plans are intended to foster a sense of common purpose within the school and the community.

Each district is required to prepare an annual report. This document summarizes the school reports, aggregates them at the district level, and develops district objectives. Additionally, each school district is required annually to submit to the state department of education a staff development report. The purpose of the report is to document district efforts to improve the competencies of its educational personnel — teachers, administrators, and para-professionals assigned to instructional duties. The program for staff development must be designed to address the educational needs identified in the school and district improvement reports.

The feature of the improvement report that differentiates South Carolina from Texas and California (and also saves the reports from being just more paperwork) is the way in which the reports are used. School principals are accountable to the district for meeting objectives developed in the school improvement plan, and districts are accountable to the state for meeting district objectives. District reports are evaluated by the state board of education. If, based upon review of the reports, the state board finds that the quality of education in a district is in serious trouble, an appointed review committee evaluates the district's educational programs. In 1985, six districts were designated as 'seriously impaired'. Review teams, appointed by the state superintendent and headed by a district superintendent visit each impaired district. Based upon its review, the team recommends strategies to improve the district's performance. District school personnel generally support the school improvement process. The superintendent in a district that had been designated as impaired believed that the attention, albeit negative, was beneficial in the long run, since it called attention to problems in the district that were beyond the district's control. Furthermore, the review mobilized state assistance and resources which the district needed. The review process calls attention to areas where reform is not taking hold. The state can target technical assistance and other resources to those areas.

A feature of school reform that differentiates South Carolina from Texas is that the reforms have decent financial support. Money is available to implement the measure's various provisions without diluting existing resources. Another distinguishing feature of reform in South Carolina is the effort to integrate reforms into the existing structure of schools. Schools were told what types of students had to be served by compensatory or remedial education programs and even what kind of progress students needed to show. But schools were left to decide what kinds of programs to establish and what mix of resources to allocate to them. Student progress is measured by a composite of tests. Some are norm referenced (measure students against one another), others are criterion referenced (measure student mastery of material). Also distinguishing South Carolina from other states is the fact that student performance is only one of a series of rather realistic measures of school effectiveness. Rather than simply reporting a series of numbers, as some states require (California, for example), South Carolina requires a report which includes planning, setting of goals and objectives, and methods for their attainment. It is naive to assume that this approach cannot also become a chase after numbers at the expense of substantive improvement. But the potential for trivializing reform by reducing it to a game of numbers is lessened if local and state roles are thoroughly integrated. If state officials only look at numbers, the incentive to districts will be to make the numbers look good. If, on the other hand, state officials take a comprehensive view of school effectiveness, schools will be forced to do the same.

Conclusions

From its inception, the educational reform effort in South Carolina strove toward consensus on reform goals and objectives and the means of attaining them. Because consensus had been achieved on major issues, educators knew about the substance of the reforms and generally agreed with them. Bargaining on major issues, particularly money, took place before implementation. Teachers and administrators who would be implementing the reforms did not have to be persuaded of their benefits or cajoled into accepting them.

One dimension of reform was an effort to focus the attention of teachers and administrators on the schools. Student testing and placement are used to determine allocation of resources and to measure outcomes. This approach is significantly different from the usual preoccupation with student outcomes. South Carolina's use of testing serves, among other ends, the purpose of targeting remedial or compensatory education services. Monitoring through school improvement plans allows the state to be informed about the performance of districts and to target assistance to those districts in need of help. In another area, teacher and administrator evaluations seek to inform individuals in both groups of their strengths and weaknesses.

The reform effort also attempts to strengthen relationships between the schools and business, industry and the general community. In an effort to solicit the support of business for a tax increase to pay for reforms, Governor Riley sought to maintain the interest of the business community beyond enactment of the reform legislation. The intent was clearly to end the isolation of public schools from business and industry. The state board of education is authorized to promote business and schools to develop 'adopt-a-school' programs. (The developer of Hilton Head, for example, adopted all the schools in Jasper and Beaufort counties.) Other ways of strengthening those relationships is through business organizations developing education foundations to fund exemplary and innovative projects in the public schools.

Some short-term effects were already evident one year after passage of the reform act. While policy-makers have expressed concern that stricter standards for student attendance, high school graduation, and participation in extra-curricular activities would increase the number of student dropouts, the opposite seems to have occurred. During 1984–85, the dropout rate declined from 5.3 per cent to 4.7 per cent, the lowest in five years. Student absences in 1984–85 were down by 30 per cent from the previous year. Remedial and compensatory education programs served over 170,000 students in 1984–85. Initial evidence from those programs indicates that students served by them made appreciable gains the standardized tests.

The real test of reform policies will be in schools such as Burke High School in Charleston. The school is all black, 75 per cent of students qualify for the free lunch program, 60 per cent of students come from single-parent homes. The school is designated a Chapter I school, which means that its students are considered disadvantaged, and over two-thirds of the students score in the bottom quartile on the California Test of Basic Skills. Parents are generally apathetic about their children's schools and community support is non-existent. Yet teachers and administrators in the school are optimistic about prospects for real reform. Whether the prevailing optimism can be sustained and translated into significant student achievement remains to be seen. Those school districts that were abandoned by whites after integration are generally the ones in greatest trouble. Yet, both teachers and administrators in those schools tend to be optimistic about reform efforts. The Education Improvement Act and the substantial increase in educational funding provided by it is regarded as an affirmation of public support for schools. Black teachers and administrators particularly regarded that as an important signal from the white majority, which only fifteen years earlier had fought to keep the state's schools segregated. Educators were willing to take the long view of reform. Most believed that the benefits would not be manifested for at least five to eight years. Several felt that the real beneficiaries of reform would be the next generation, the children of those children who are now in school.

Notes and References

1. Larry Cuban 'Transforming the frog into a prince: Effective schools research, policy, and practice at the district level', *Harvard Education Review*, 54, (1984).
2. This view is consistent with scientific philosophy that is premised on the idea that truth exists in the universe and waits to be discovered. The contrasting view is best expressed by St. Exupery's aphorism that 'great truths are created, not discovered'.
3. See W. Norton Grubb *et. al .*, *The Initial Effects of House Bill 72 on Texas Public Schools: The Challenge of Equity and Effectiveness*, (Austin: Lyndon B. Johnson School of Public Affairs, The University of Texas, 1985); and William C. Bednar, Jr. 'A survey of the Texas reform package: House Bill 72', *St. Mary's Law Journal*, 16, (1985).

4. Select Committee on Public Education '*Recommendations*' (Austin, TX: State Printing Office. 19 April 1984).
5. *Ibid.*, page 20.
6. *Ibid.*, page 19.
7. See Raymond E. Callahan *Education and the Cult of Efficiency*, (Chicago: University of Chicago Press, 1962).
8. See Callahan *op. cit.*; also David B. Tyack *The One Best System*, (Cambridge, Mass.: Harvard Press, 1974) p. 143.
9. *Idem*, page 26.
10. *Idem*, page 22.
11. *Idem*, page 21.
12. *Idem*, page 23.
13. A major force behind the equalization effort was the threat of a major lawsuit by the Mexican American Legal Defense and Education Fund (MALDEF). The suit, *Edgewood v. Bynum*, filed in May of 1984 was essentially a restatement of the *Rodriguez* case in 1871. The legislature thought that by addressing the wealth disparities among rich and poor districts, the law suit would become moot. For a thorough discussion of the equalizing provisions of HB 72 see Grubb, Note #3. Also Deborah A. Verstegen, Richard Hooker and Nolan Estes 'A comprehensive shift in educational policy-making: Texas education reform legislation', in *The Fiscal, Legal, and Political Aspects of State Reform of Elementary and Secondary Education*, (San Francisco, CA: Ballinger, 1986).
14. *Idem*, page 25.
15. Judith Warren Little *School Success and Staff Development: The Role of Staff Development in Urban Desegregated Schools*, (Washington, DC: National Institute of Education, 1981).
16. *House Bill 72*, Sec. 13.321. Emphasis added.
17. Bednar *op. cit.*, page 827.
18. Bednar *op. cit.*, page 824.
19. Bednar *op. cit.*, page 825.
20. Grubb *et al.*, *op. cit.*, page 53.
21. *Texas Education Code*, Sec. 21.103.
22. Grubb *et al.*, *op. cit.* page 55.
23. Paul Berman and Milbrey Wallin McLaughlin *Federal Programs Supporting Educational Change, Vol. VIII: Implementing and Sustaining Innovations*, (Santa Monica, CA: Rand Corp., May 1978).
24. Bednar *op cit.*, page 832.
25. *Ibid*, page 832.
26. *Ibid*, page 112.
27. *Ibid*, page 116.
28. *Ibid*, page 116.
29. Robert Fairbanks and Rick Boeck. 'Reform is here for schools, but are schools ready for reform?', *California Journal*, (October, 1983).
30. Fairbanks and Boeck *op. cit*, page 390.
31. *Ibid*, page 391.
32. Honig changed his tune soon after the election. He argued for a nearly $2 billion increase for schools, arguing that the schools could not improve without a massive infusion of money.

33. Larry Cuban 'School reform by remote control: SB 813 in California', *Phi Delta Kappan*, (November, 1984) pages 213–215.
34. Fairbanks and Boeck *op. cit.*, page 393.
35. *Ibid*, page 393.
36. Loren Kaye *Making the Grade? Assessing School District Progress on SB 813*, (Sacramento, CA: California Tax Foundation, 1985) page 11.
37. Cited in Kaye *op. cit.*, page 13.
38. Judith Shulman, George St. Clair and Judith Warren Little *Expanded Teacher Roles: Mentors and Masters* (San Francisco: Far West Laboratory for Education Research and Development, 1984).
39. Shulman *et al.*, *op. cit.*, page 15.
40. Shulman *et al.*, *op. cit.*
41. Shulman *et al.*, *op. cit.*, page 11.
42. Shulman *et al.*, page 32.
43. California State Legislature *Analysis of the Budget Bill: A Report of the Joint Budget Committee, 1984–85.*, (Sacramento: Office of the Legislative Analyst, 1984), pages 1440–46.
44. Paul Berman and Dan Weiler *Improving Student Performance in California*, (Berkeley, CA: California Business Roundtable, 1983).
45. Quoted in Kaye *op. cit.*, page 16.
46. *Idem*, pages 1440–1446.
47. Kaye *op. cit.*, page 26.
48. This is calculated based on 1 minute x 5 passing times x 180 days. Kaye *op. cit.*, page 27.
49. Edward Bridges *The Incompetent Teacher*, (Lewes: Falmer Press, 1986).
50. Fairbanks and Boeck *op. cit.*, page 393.
51. See chapter 3 for a discussion of the implementation of Quality Indicators.
52. Fairbanks and Boeck *op. cit.*, page 393.
53. US Education Department, Office of Planning, Budget, and Evaluation, Planning and Evaluation Service, January 1985.
54. South Carolina, Office of the Governor and State Department of Education *The Public Viewpoint: Education in South Carolina*, (1983).
55. William J. Blough 'Governing South Carolina's public schools', in Charlie B. Tyer and Cole Blease Graham, Jr. (Eds) *Local Government in South Carolina, Vol. I: The Governmental Landscape*, (Columbia, S.C.: Bureau of Governmental Research and Service; University of South Carolina, 1985).
56. William J. Blough *op. cit.* page 111. See also John Norton, 'Our schools, A special report', *The State*, Part I (15 January 1984); Part II (22 January 1984), Part III (29 January 1984). Also John Norton *The South Carolina Public Schools Sourcebook*, (Columbia, SC: Southeast Public Education Program, American Friends Service Committee, 1980).
57. Paul Hubbard. Quoted in the *Washington Post*, (4 September 1984).
58. *South Carolina Code*. Section 59–20–60 (4) (a).

5 Between Planning And Politics: How States Manage Educational Excellence

The Landscape of Educational Reform

If the state education reform effort since the Commission on Educational Excellence issued its report in 1983 is measured in terms of sheer numbers, the overall effort would surely be pronounced a success. The level of activity is unprecedented in the nation's history. Over fifteen states have enacted comprehensive reforms. New programs and initiatives abound; and few areas of institutional life in the schools remain untouched. But what, in fact, has changed? Has the agenda of educational excellence that was proposed in *A Nation At Risk* been broadly embraced? The volume of state policy initiatives suggest that a new agenda has, indeed, been embraced. But the important question is whether it will significantly alter the structures of schooling and the lives of students. In this chapter, we examine what has changed and what not, and offer an analytical framework for assessing the significance of the changes.

One way in which the terrain has changed is that educational issues — as distinguished from social issues discussed in the context of education — have gained pre-eminence on many state legislative agendas. Not since the wave of post-Sputnik reforms has education been so prominent nationally. Suddenly, governors, state legislators, and state education departments are vying with one another over educational policy. The Council of State Governments, the National Conference of State Legislatures and the National Governors' Association have all given education high priority on their respective agendas. The National Governors' Association, in fact, has created various task forces to hold hearings on state policy options for education reform and intends to monitor state actions for several years to come.

There has also been an increase in the national consciousness about education. Television specials have focused on effective schools. The Governor of Texas, Mark White, has appeared on CBS's 'Face the Nation' and national nightly news programs to defend the state's 'no pass, no play' regulation. *'Parade'* magazine dedicated an entire issue to a survey of teacher attitudes. And where five years ago the focus of media attention was on the failure of schools, the emphasis has definitely shifted to reforming schools.

A variety of factors — the overwhelmingly favorable public reception of *A Nation at Risk*, the pressure of foreign economic competition, and the media attention given to the decline in academic standards and student achievement — have created an inchoate national consensus on education policy. As we examined educational reform initiatives enacted by state legislatures, we were struck by the similarities among them. Not only do many share similar titles, but specific statutory provisions are also quite similar. Common definition of the problem of educational mediocrity and common policy solutions have resulted in homogenizing educational policy nationally. In terms of broad state policy goals — curriculum, student performance, teacher and administrator competence, high school graduation requirements, college entrance requirements, and length of the instructional day and year — disparities among state school systems have narrowed. On the state level, for example, Texas and South Carolina both have statewide policies about classroom interruptions and student participation in extracurricular activities. South Carolina requires schools to provide programs for students in need of remediation; Texas mandates a common curriculum in all subjects; and Texas and Tennessee have moved toward a common evaluation mechanism for all teachers. Not only have reforms increased standardization and uniformity among school districts in states, but nationally as well. The effect of this phenomenon of reform is perhaps most obvious in the Southeast, where the educational achievement of students historically has been the lowest among states in the nation and where educational standards and practices traditionally were matters of local discretion. There, change has been most dramatic.

Across the nation, educational standards have been ratcheted upwards. Academic requirements have increased: students must spend more time in school, take more credits for graduation, and enroll in more 'solid' courses such as science, math, and foreign languages; in many schools, new courses in the use of computers have been added. To meet higher academic expectations, more dedicated and more highly qualified teachers are needed. This is why states have tried both to make it harder to become a teacher and more attractive to remain one. In order to provide necessary leadership to the schools, principals must acquire new skills consistent with their new roles as instructional leaders, as opposed to their traditional roles as managers.

Governance has also changed. According to one school board member in Texas 'The legislature has taken over and tried to control everything in God Almighty's world'.[1] Dennis Doyle and Terry Hartle, in their assessment of the school reform movement, suggest that 'the process of implementing the new laws seems likely to shift the balance of power even further from local education agencies to state governments'.[2] Others see the issue less starkly. David S. Seeley, former Assistant United States Commissioner of Education, believes that 'too many people make the assumption that educational power is a zero-sum game; if somebody wins, then somebody has to lose'. On the contrary, Seeley suggests, considerable power exists that neither state nor local officials have exercised.[3]

In addition to shifts in state-local governance relationships, the participation of new actors in educational policymaking has broadened the roster of individuals in governance. The national school reform effort has been fueled largely by lay groups. In California, for example, the participation of powerful business-industry coalitions in the process of educational reform was particularly influential in diluting the power traditionally wielded by teachers' unions. In Texas particularly, but also in other states, educational reform became a test of political strength between newly formed business coalitions, on the one hand, and entrenched education coalitions, on the other. The result is that educational policy is no longer the satrapy of educators.

As politicians have poached on policy territory that had traditionally belonged exclusively to educators, educators have moved into politics. This is not news in states like California, but it is novel in Texas where educational reforms have prompted athletic coaches and administrators to form political action committees. The groups state that they generally support the state's reform measure, but are concerned about 'the inflexible requirements in the law as related to discipline and the career ladder'.[4]

While it is too early for a conclusive evaluation of student outcomes, there are signs that state reform policies are having some positive effects. In Texas, for example, fewer football players were declared ineligible because of failing grades during the second year of the 'no pass, no play' rule because coaches organized tutorials for athletes to ensure their sports eligibility. In South Carolina, student attendance increased dramatically as a result of a state mandate limiting the number of allowable absences, and students in remedial programs have shown considerable progress in catching up with other students. In many states, academically promising students can attend academies to learn special skills in math, science, and computers.

One of the definite benefits of the reform movement has been to provide additional resources to schools. Even though no national data are available to determine the cost of reform, revenue increases in various educational catagories in different states suggests sizable increases. California, for example, increased state school spending by approximately $1 billion in each of three successive years, beginning with 1983–84. That is approximately a 10 per cent annual increase, well above the rate of inflation and the size of previous increases. New York increased school spending by about $1 billion, about 4.5 per cent annually, over two years.

On the other hand, the educational landscape has changed in some ways that were unanticipated by, and may be troublesome to, reformers. One of these unintended consequences is renewed reliance on courts for resolving educational policy disputes. Reform efforts have sparked legal challenges to specific reform provisions in several states. In Florida, for instance, teacher organizations challenged the state's merit pay plan. Teachers unions in California have gone to court over statutory changes in personnel practices. In Texas, public interest groups representing ethnic minorities have filed suit over competency testing of prospective teachers. Parents first sought temporary restraining orders from the courts to enjoin districts from enforcing the 'no pass, no play' rule, and then sought a decision to overturn the rule.

Reform has also made the educational system more bureaucratized. As new rules and regulations have proliferated, the number of individuals administering their implementation has grown apace. Texas, Tennessee and Florida created new state structures for teacher placement and evaluation. Arkansas and Texas developed new tests to assess their respective teachers' competencies. Some states have established new departments in their education agencies to monitor district reform activities and have formed standing oversight committees to review the activities of their state education agencies. There are instances of monitors monitoring the monitors as well as a proliferation of reporting requirements. Those skeptical of state reform efforts see many of the reforms as a paper chase after meaningless data.

There has also been deliberate evasion of policy goals. In

Newark, New Jersey, for example, a merit pay pilot program was rescinded by the state following allegations that merit pay was used to reward the union faithful. A high school math teacher and girls' basketball coach were dismissed in Texas for selling high grades to students. In Chico, California, high school seniors tried to blackmail a district into giving them special privileges — an overnight trip to a beach resort and a paved student parking lot — in return for their taking a state mandated test (the CAP) seriously.

The Limits of Reform

Not everyone agrees with the palliative effects of reform. Some doubt the capacity of reforms to affect very deeply long-established institutional arrangements; others see in the reforms some unanticipated and unhappy results that may, in fact, work against the ideal of educational excellence. The authors of *The Shopping Mall High School* conclude that:

> ... the metaphor (of the shopping mall high school) rather understates the many complex and carefully balanced bargains that keep these overworked organizations running — and running in a way that seems to please most of their clients and constituents. If we knew nothing else about the schools, we would suppose it unlikely that the last wave of criticism and reform would change this pattern of accommodation.[5]

The realities of organizational life in the schools often supersede the exigencies of reform. A certain number of teachers are needed to manage classrooms, for example, and if there are insufficient numbers of credentialed teachers — as in California and Texas — others must be found, regardless of their caliber. So too, as efforts to increase student enrollment in academic programs create a demand for teachers in those areas, displaced shop and physical education teachers are reassigned as English and math instructors. Even if those teachers have the best intentions to do a good job, their lack of academic qualifications is a serious obstacle.

Tightening standards for entry into teaching and diluting protections that make it virtually impossible to fire an incompetent teacher may make a difference. But can the difference be more than marginal? Obvious incompetents may be more easily screened out, but what effect will reforms have on the average teacher? A recent national poll of teacher attitudes is not encouraging. Only 40 per cent of teachers are satisfied with their jobs compared to 52 per cent of the total workforce. Forty per cent of teachers are more negative now about teaching than when they first started. And one-third of teachers would leave their jobs even if the salary were no more than they presently earn.[6]

More important, the views of teachers regarding the success of state reform efforts is discouraging. Over half of the teachers surveyed thought that strict curriculum and higher grading standards have not improved the education that students are receiving. One wonders what effect educational reforms can have if the majority of those who implement them doubt their efficacy.

The ubiquity of educational reform efforts in this century must be viewed against the capacity of the educational system to resist significant change. That is why some observers remain skeptical of the effects of reform on the quality of schooling. As policy-makers have attempted to narrow local discretion by promoting uniformity and standardization, a narrowing of educational objectives has occurred. Within states, wide disparities in expenditures have narrowed and that is all for the good. But the negative aspect of this phenomenon may be the reduction of learning to rote, standardization, basics, and test scores.

The national penchant for relying upon the schools to save the country from whatever ails it fostered the conditions that allowed the shopping mall high school to flourish. As a result, schools lack a clear public policy focus, and they also lack a clear institutional focus. Schools are expected to promote social mobility, political stability, and economic growth. As institutions, they provide childcare, counseling services, and vocational and academic preparation. They are also called upon to imbue children with a variety of social and athletic skills. Consequently, schools eschew values, judgments about what is correct or incorrect, appropriate for study or inappropriate. The absence of values is manifested in organizational incoherence and absence of organizational purpose. Schools tend to be highly fragmented places where teachers teach, counselors counsel, and administrators administer. The structure of schooling has much in common with a factory assembly line. While such an arrangement may serve the purpose of accommodating widely disparate needs in a pluralistic society, it is incompatible with the goal of substantially improving the overall quality of schooling in the nation. The fragmented character of schools is a stark contrast to the conditions that foster excellence — a sense of community, shared purpose, common values and mission, and an understanding of the cultural values on which education is built. Substantive reform depends on a much clearer sense of what is most important to teach and learn, and why, and how it can best be done. Mandating in minute detail what needs to be done, as is done in states like Texas, is useless if teachers fail to grasp the instructional purpose.

Implementation Strategies and Policy Outcomes

The results of this latest spate of reforms are mixed. Higher standards have been mandated in nearly all states and corresponding policies have been promulgated to effect them. A greater public commitment to educational reform is also evident. Critics argue that the changes are merely superficial, not likely to have much impact on well-established organizational arrangements. Both assessments are correct. But missing from both perspectives is a critical question: do differences among states in how they manage education reform have any systematic relationship to policy outcomes? Do some strategies for reform simply exacerbate the lack of coherence that characterizes much of the existing educational system? Do other strategies promote institutional arrangements that encourage educational excellence?

There is little empirical evidence to help state policymakers in their reform efforts.[7]

It is still not clear which implementation strategies are most effective because few researchers have investigated the connections between strategies and outcomes. Most researchers have recognized the tangled complexity of such diverse elements as context, roles, individual, organizational factors such as size, history, and culture, quality of leadership at both district and school levels, timing, and other critical determinants of successful implementation. Beyond recognizing this complexity, few researchers have proceeded further than to construct inventories and taxonomies of essential points in establishing causal relationships between strategies and outcomes.[8]

While it would be overly ambitious to argue that a clear cause-and-effect relationship exists between implementation strategies and outcomes, the case studies indicate that implementation strategies are related to policy outcomes.

The Texas, California, and South Carolina studies show that there are, indeed, discernible differences in how states manage school reform. Texas exemplifies a reform strategy that relies on top-down mandates, centralized authority, as well as on standardization and uniformity in both substance and process. California's reform strategy depends on artificially created market incentives to promote school districts to change their behavior. California's approach is similar to Texas in that policy formulation is highly centralized, but differs in that implementation is highly decentralized, subject to state financial incentives and local bargaining. South Carolina's management strategy, by contrast, is 'bottom-up'. The distinguishing attributes of this strategy are consensus on policy goals, discretionary authority in implementation, and a strong commitment to state goals.

Rules and Styles of Decision Making

Rational Planning

The philosophical underpinnings of top-down reform strategies are rooted in the legacy of eighteenth century Rationalism. The contemporary inheritors of that tradition are the social technocrats 'who believe that some people in the society are wise and informed enough to ameliorate its problems and guide social change with a high degree of success'.[9] The notable features of this management strategy include a high degree of centralization, uniformity, and formal authority. This approach to policy implementation assumes that organizational units in the implementation process are linked in essentially hierarchical relationships. This assumption has two corollaries: the closer one is to the source of the policy, the greater is one's authority and influence; and the ability of complex systems to respond to problems depends on the establishment of clear lines of authority and control.[10]

Rational planning focuses on policy areas that tend to centralize control and are easily manipulated by policymakers: funding formulas, formal organizational structures; authority relationships among administrative units; regulations; and administrative controls (budget, planning, and evaluation requirements). It takes but a short leap from the proposition that there are single, best solutions to complex social problems to the conclusion that bureaucracies can be tightly controlled to carry out the mandates of social planners.

The case study of how education reform has been implemented in Texas illustrates that the assumptions upon which hierarchical planning is built do not hold for educational excellence. Organizational units in education are not linked in hierarchical relationships but are part of a 'loosely-coupled' structure of bureaucracies.[11] Consequently, proximity to the source of policy may enhance influence and authority over policy decision-making without having any effect on how those decisions are implemented. As the reform effort in Texas shows, there are no clear lines of authority and control. Thus, policies, cannot be controlled by central planners and policy coordinators as they move through the policy pipeline.

It is precisely the element of central coordination and planning that establishes the limits of this strategy.

> To the extent that the implementation process is dominated by regulation, formal organizational structure, and management control, one would expect problems of complexity to increase. The tighter the structure of hierarchical relationships, the greater the number of checks and decision points required to assure compliance, the more opportunities for diversion and delay, the greater the reliance of subordinates on superiors for guidance, and the lower the reliance on individual judgment and problem solving ability.[12]

In striving for uniformity and standardization through regulation and control, rational planning ironically achieves the opposite result — fragmentation. This fragmentation is manifested in various ways. Policy development is separated from implementation. One group plans policies, another oversees their execution, and a third actually executes them. Policy decision and policy execution are separated: those who make the decisions are not these who implement them. One manifestation of the resulting slippage is when efforts to promote teaching excellence are turned into a parodies of teaching — an obsession with portfolios, for example, to justify merit increases. Top-down implementation fragments the process of education by dividing it into discrete policies. Excellence is not seen as a concept, but as a conglomeration of activities that theoretically add up to excellence.

Rational planning encourages functional fragmentation. Teachers, administrators, counselors, and students all have their assigned roles. English teachers teach one set of skills, math teachers another, and history teachers a third. Learning is compartmentalized by subjects and mastery of skills within those subjects. There is little sense of cohesion. In Texas, for example, the school curriculum is divided into a large number of elements, each of which is to be taught. The predominant focus of policy is not on strengthening the capacity of schools to improve, but on the bits and pieces of the instructional process.

One of the ironies of rational planning is that the more policy planners strive for centralization and uniformity, the more rules and regulations proliferate, and the more policy makers rely on formal structures of authority for administration and compliance, the less likely they are to achieve it.[13] What is missing is an organizational context for decisionmaking that emphasizes a vision of the entire educational landscape rather than narrow views, here and there, of pieces of that landscape. Because rational planning is predicated on the assumption that there is a single, best policy solution to a particular problem, consensus building is absent from the process.

The absence of consensus not only makes conflict inevitable, but also increases the cost of resolving conflict. While conflict is a healthy and necessary feature of democratic politics, political theorists also emphasize the need for means of conflict resolution.[14] Conflict inheres in the nature of hierarchical policy implementation. Rational planning, as illustrated by Texas, eschews consensus in the process of policy definition. As a result, many of those who must live with the policies disagree with them. Moreover, hierarchical planning does not rely on informal bargaining arenas and on informal means of dispute resolution. As a result, conflict resolution must depend on formal, often adversarial, forums. Changing formal structures necessitates formal processes. Seeking policy changes engenders transaction costs that drain resources from the principal effort of schooling.

A critical feature of hierarchical policy implementation is how planners define excellence. The tendency is to regard educational excellence as a series of discrete problems to be solved. The perspective is not broad — on how to strengthen and improve institutions — but narrow — on how to effect changes in specific areas of institutional life. No one knows 'how to grow effective schools', as Larry Cuban puts it. As much as policy-makers may wish for it, there is no technical rationality to direct school people in how to achieve excellence. Nor is there agreement on definitions: concepts such as 'climate' and 'instructional leadership' may be interpreted in various ways. And, understandings of effectiveness are too narrow. Measures of student progress, for example, generally rely upon standardized tests and are based on low order skills in math and reading.[15] Measures of teacher effectiveness, similarly, are based upon their capacity to teach to a standardized curriculum. Consequently, rational planners find themselves attempting to achieve policy goals that are based on technological rationality that is, at best, only vaguely understood and rarely replicated.

Political Interaction

In contrast to top-down policy implementation strategies, a bottom-up approach shifts the policy perspective from reliance on formal control and regulation which flows from a central authority to informal devices of authority that rely on delegation, discretion, and dispersal of authority. As a management strategy, this approach

> stresses the dispersal of control and concentrates on factors that can only be indirectly influenced by policy-makers: knowledge and problem solving ability of lower-level administrators; incentive structures that operate on the subjects of policy; bargaining relationships among political actors at various levels of the implementation process; and strategic use of funds to affect discretionary choices.[16]

The antithesis of rational planning is policy through political or social interaction. Rather than seeking a single, best solution to problems, this approach to policy development and implementation recognizes that there are many ways to reach similar ends. This strategy is cognizant of the various conditions that influence organizational behavior, and rather than prescribe specific palliatives, it stresses the need for variability, flexibility, and problem solving. Such an interactive approach to decision making assumes that there are no correct solutions discernible through analysis. The interactive model of decision making establishes a process for problem solving instead of proposing single, best solution to a problem.[17]

The difference between the two strategies is illustrated by how Texas and South Carolina approached policy development. In Texas, issues were defined by a committee of school reformers, while in South Carolina, issues were defined through a process that drew upon broad-based participation. Most important, South Carolina tended to focus on policy goals and outcomes, leaving matters of how to best achieve those goals to local school districts. Simply stated, a bottom-up strategy aims at strengthening local institutions and encouraging local innovation and experimentation by allowing variation. On an organizational level, a bottom-up strategy concentrates on generating among staff shared values about what the school should be, creating a team spirit, and cultivating mutual trust through collaborative decision-making on school issues.

A defining characteristic of bottom-up reform is that it does not create a regulatory structure to implement reforms, but aims at the integration of reform policies into existing organizational structures. South Carolina, for example, allowed schools to specify how they would attend to students in need of compensatory or remedial education. Policy coordination is through consensus, not, as with top-down reform, through external mandate and regulation. The element of consensus becomes a means of policy coordination and self-regulation.

Education reform cannot engineer outcomes through implementation of specific policies for there is no available technology. It does, however, involve creating organizations with characteristics which foster educational excellence. That effort is best accomplished through bottom-up efforts.

Market Incentives

The creation of financial incentives to promote state educational reform initiatives is unique to California. This approach to policy concentrates policy development at the state level, but lets their implementation be bargained over locally. Although rules and regulations are in place, adherence is a matter of local choice. That choice, in turn, is colored by bargaining relations between local school officials and teacher unions.

The role of the state authorities is twofold. The state defines the policy goals and develops guidelines for their implementation; it also defines the boundaries of the market. For example, state regulations broadly prescribe the elements of the mentor teachers program and then generally specify the bargaining context that determines the program's various elements on the local level. Similarly, in the area of personnel reforms, districts can make changes in areas of personnel management, but they must implement those enabling provisions.

As a strategy for school reform, the *laissez faire* approach shows mixed results. On the one hand, it can promote cooperation, working toward common goals, problem solving, and flexibility — conditions necessary to effective schools. On the other hand, such a strategy opens a door to opportunistic compliance, evasion of state policy goals, and non-compliance. Schools extending the time between classes in order to qualify for additional funds illustrates opportunistic compliance. The permissive nature of this strategy, combined with the absence of accountability measures, is what differentiates this from a bottom-up implementation strategy. In South Carolina, for example, schools are free to structure remedial and compensatory education programs according to their needs. If schools fail to show results, however, they invite state intervention. A comparable intervention strategy does not exist in California.

Styles of Decision Making and Reform Strategies

Educational excellence is fostered by a complex mixture of cultural and institutional factors. It is not likely to be cultivated by disparate policies that aim at various pieces of the educational process. Merit pay for teachers, for example, can be effective, but only within the broader context of the school and community. A study of the effects of merit pay for teachers[18] shows that merit increases bear scant relationship to their presumed effects — as an incentive to better teaching. Merit pay can be a positive inducement to teachers but only in relationship to the whole — as an affirmation of school and community support. Requiring students to take more academic classes means little if the substance of those classes is thin and lacking in rigor. Similarly there is no benefit to keeping students in classes longer if little learning takes place in those classes. The purpose of reform policies should be to create the kinds of institutional arrangements and organizational structures that promote educational excellence. Whether school reforms take hold in South Carolina, Texas or California depends on degree to which that can be accomplished.

Enacting new rules for schools to follow may just add to the baggage that already overburdens the system. Reforms must create a sense of coherence and direction for schools as institutions. Reform policies may result in producing a crop of new teachers who are better prepared to teach their subjects. But what will prepare them for the indifference, monotony, incoherence, and rampant directionlessness of the institution itself, the jealousy of colleagues, the blandness of the architecture, and the spiritual sterility of the environment? A school must set a certain tone — which is as real as the classrooms themselves — that will greet the students. That tone, organizational ethos, determines the character of the school. It sets the expectation for excellence or failure. But it is created by individuals working in schools, not by bureaucratic mandates that emanate from distant places.

Reforms will fail if they do not prompt schools to forge for themselves an organizational identity. As long as teachers think of themselves as employees in a shopping mall or day care center, police station or hospital, where they simply put in their hours with no thought to definition of what it is they are trying to achieve, schools will not change. Schools need an organizational focus and it is teachers, parents and administrators who decide what that focus ought to be and how to define it in the daily life of the school. That cannot be done through directives and regulations from state legislatures and centralized bureaucracies. It can only be done in the schools, by school personnel creating the kinds of organizations that can engender, as organizations, a vision of what education is and ought to be. Since fragmentation is one of the features of schools, it follows that more hierarchically imposed regulations, no matter how well intentioned they may be, exacerbate that fragmentation.

One possible organizational rearrangement to counter fragmentation might be to break schools, especially high schools, into smaller units, even if they occupy the same building. The shopping mall nature of schools is supported by the sheer size and organizational disparateness of many schools. Large size is generally attended by functional separation. Administrators are separated from counselors and teachers who are separated by departments or grade levels. Students move from one classroom to another, from one activity to another. The structure itself encourages only superficial contact between adults and students, and even between one group of adults and another, and hinders the kind of interaction that builds shared goals, common values, and a sense of purpose.[19]

Specialization, like school size, engenders fragmentation and should, for that reason, be discouraged. Teachers, counselors and administrators, all functioning in their own professional niches, discourage organizational integration. While most school people would agree that schools cannot and should not be arranged like assembly lines, schools persist in arranging themselves just so. Everyone should teach, advise, coach sports, direct a play. Teachers and students should see one another in contexts other than the classroom. The more time that teachers and students spend together in different roles, the greater the potential for creating relationships that foster learning. Similarly, everyone should be an administrator in the true sense of that word — an instructional leader. The idea of administrators as managers is incompatible with the concept of purposive decision-making. Everyone must share in establishing goals, priorities and must equally share in taking responsibility for achieving those goals.

A common feature of schools as they are presently organized is the absence of responsibility. Teachers blame parents, a lax home environment, and mass media for the suffocating mediocrity of schools. School personnel also like to blame politicians and the public for lack of adequate funding. Politicians, in turn, like to blame teachers and administrators who, politicians claim, pursue narrow, selfish interests (as opposed to the high-minded interest of politicians, one presumes) at the expense of students. Embedded in this latter criticism is the notion that teachers. administrators, and school district trustees have selfishly allowed education to deteriorate behind the backs of politicians.

These positions are easy to take when education is such a fragmented process. But just as no one group can be legitimately singled out for blame, no one group can be targeted for reform. Fragmented responses to an already fragmented system only exacerbate the problem. For even if the attribution of failure is correct — student test scores are low, some teachers are incompetent in the mastery of even the most basic academic skills — that does not mean that the positive side of that equation necessarily leads to substantive reform. In the calculus of excellence, simply improving test scores, eliminating incompetent teachers from the classroom, and the like may resolve a particular problem but will not promote the goal of educational excellence. The responsibility for excellence should reside in the schools, not in state legislatures.

Schools as organizations must provide a maturing process for teachers as well as for students. There are several ways to promote that. Much of the drudgery of teaching has to be eliminated. As one teacher stated 'Because my students really do need the drill work of vocabulary and grammar doesn't mean that I have to grade it'. Teachers need to think and plan, not just perform mindless tasks. Teachers must do things that make them proficient at teaching. Much of the drudgery and routine of school works against that. Instead of spending tens of millions of dollars to extend the school day by several minutes as California did, for example, money could be spent on hiring college students to assist in much of the routine work that teachers presently perform.

Teachers need to be able to achieve, compete, and be held to standards. Tenure, for example, ought to be more of an achievement than it presently is. And while there should be some kind of rank as well as legitimate criteria for measuring proficiency, achievement, and competence. Competence comes with a sense of achievement and status. If real reform can only be achieved by changing the institutional nature of schools, what then is the role of the state in managing the reform process? The first observation is that state efforts should be targeted at strengthening schools as organizations in the manner we have suggested above. In this context the role of the state is to establish professional standards and expectations and to provide support and to nurture organizational characteristics that foster excellence. The Carnegie Commission has already proposed a massive restructuring of teacher work roles and training.[20] However, just as states regulate the medical, legal, and other professions without presuming to tell lawyers how many cases they need to win, or doctors what medication to prescribe to patients, states should regulate the teaching profession without intruding into the process of teaching. The role of the state would be to 'articulate principles of institutional design and institutional diagnosis'.[21] An appropriate state management strategy would be to create a capacity to determine a harmonious fit between state control agencies and schools: what blend of cognitive, organizational, and political resources schools require for the realization of their purpose.

If states are serious about improving educational quality and striving for excellence, they must create the appropriate context in which that can take place. That effort will require fundamental redefinition of various organizational roles. The dichotomized view of local versus state control, for example, is inappropriate and anachronistic if institutional change becomes the focus of reform. The distribution between state and local authority is no longer a zero-sum game over specific policy decisions but a cooperative effort aimed at enhancing organizational competence. The effort has to be centered on enhancing institutional effectiveness. The history of educational reform in America is full of innovative strategies that became routine in the process of bureaucratic aging.

Conclusion

Achieving excellence in the nation's schools is unlikely in the absence of a radical reformulation of American education policy. As long as American education policy continues in the tradition of past policies that focus on the good of individuals or groups at the expense of institutions, real educational reform will not occur. The Great Society reforms as well as the romantic revival of the Individual in the 1960s and 1970s made the individual the focus of public policy. Educational policies regarding early childhood education, compensatory education, bilingual programs, services for the handicapped, gender equity focused on groups of individuals that were in need of special education services. The purpose of those policies was not to strengthen the schools as educational institutions and to better define the institutional role of schools in American culture. Quite to the contrary, many of the Great Society school reforms betokened a deep suspicion of all public institutions, including schools.

In retrospect, policy-makers treated schools as though they were made of silly-putty and could be twisted into cogenial shapes to suit specific policy needs. Compensatory education programs responded to the perceived inattention of schools to the needs of poor, and generally minority, educationally disadvantaged children. Schools could be made to provide special services to only those students, so those students could play catch-up with other, presumably more advantaged students. Programs for the learning disabled and the handicapped similarly targeted the needs of special categories of students and required schools to respond to those needs. Whether the problem was perceived to be social justice or equal protection under the law, the response to any problem was to create a new set of policies. Policies proliferated with problems, and there was certainly no shortage of problems as social reformers were quick to point out.

Public institutions were simply the agents of this reform agenda. At the same time, public institutions, and the schools among them, were regarded by many social reformers with a good deal of suspicion. Institutions were seen (and certainly not without some justification) to represent vested interest that were opposed to change, particularly since change augured a redistribution of public benefits. Strong mistrust of institutions, on the one hand, and romantic faith in the capacity of the individual, on the other, contributed to the fragmentation that characterizes the schools today. To the extent that the present reform efforts continue that tradition, policies that have been promulgated to foster excellence will just add to the array of policies that currently fracture the institutional purpose of schools.

In some respects, the current wave of educational reform repeats the history of past reform efforts. Policies intended to foster educational excellence are again targeted to special groups. Only this time, teachers, administrators, counselors, and even trustees are the targets of reform. Again, reform efforts eschew institutional change in favor of marginal changes. In a general sense, the aim of reform is the individual or groups of individuals. If only teachers were paid more, they would be more productive. If administrators were better trained, they would be more effective. The intent of much of the school reform effort is to make individuals better off. This is a different policy perspective from that which would make institutions better off.

There is no denying that the elements of reform — adequate pay and a career structure for teachers, school curricula that have intellectual and academic integrity, and many others — are essential pieces in the overall effort. But absent some organizational coherence to those reforms, they retain their cafeteria character. To give them coherence, however, prompts a fundamentally different view of educational policy. The issue is an old one. Do we put public good ahead of private good? From another perspective, the question is whether institutions define and serve the common good, or whether institutions are agents to empower private wants.

Notes and References

1. *Education Week*, 8 May 1985.
2. Dennis P. Doyle and Terry W. Hartle *Excellence in Education: The States Take Charge*, (Washington, DC: American Enterprise Institute, 1985).
3. *Education Week*, 8 May 1985.
4. *Education Week*, 8 January 1986.
5. Arthur G. Powell, Eleanor Farrar and David K. Cohen *The Shopping Mall High School*, (Boston: Houghton Mifflin, 1985), page 301.
6. *Parade*, 1 December 1985.
7. See, for example, Richard Elmore 'Backward mapping: Implementation research and policy decisions', *Political Science Quarterly*, 94, (1979–80) and 'Organizational models of social program implementation', *Public Policy*, 26 (Spring 1978). Richard F. Elmore and Milbrey W. McLaughlin 'Strategic choice in federal education policy: The compliance assistance trade-off', in Ann Liebermann and Milbrey W. McLaughlin (Eds) *Policy-making in Education*, (Chicago: University of Chicago Press, 1982).
8. Larry Cuban 'Transforming the frog into a prince: Effective schools research, policy and practice and the district level, *Harvard Educational Review*, 54, (May 1984) page 140.
9. Charles E. Lindblom *Politics and Markets*, (New York: Basic Books, 1977) p. 249.
10. Richard F. Elmore 'Backward mapping: Implementation research and policy decisions', *Political Science Quarterly*, Vol. 94 No. 4, (Winter 1979–80) p. 605.
11. John Meyer 'Organizational factors affecting legalization in education', in David L. Kirp and Donald N. Jensen (Eds) *School Days, Rule Days*, (London: Falmer Press, 1986).
12. Elmore *op. cit.*, page 608.
13. *Ibid.*

14. See E. E. Schattschneider *The Semisovereign People*, (Hinsdale, Ill.; Dryden Press, 1960); and Pendelton Herring *The Politics of Democracy*, (New York.: W.W. Norton, 1940).
15. Larry Cuban *op. cit.*, p. 131.
16. Elmore *op. cit.*, page 605.
17. Lindblom *op. cit.*
18. David K. Cohen and Richard Murnane 'The merits of merit pay', *Public Interest*, 80 (Summer 1985).
19. This is not a new idea. See, for example, 'Reformers, radicals and romantics', in Ravitch, *op. cit.* Reform proposals during the 1960s to create schools-within-schools and the like were not intended to strengthen schools as educational institutions, but just the opposite, to break down the institutional authority of schools. See also Ann Swidler *Organization Without Authority: Dilemmas of Social Control in Free Schools*, (Cambridge, Mass: Harvard University Press, 1979).
20. Carnegie ... See also Holmes Group and Commons Commission.
21. Philippe Nonet and Phillip Selznick *Law and Society in Transition: Toward Responsive Law*, (New York: Harper and Row, 1978), page 111.

6 Conclusion: A Theory of Institutional Support

The school reform movement is peopled at one extreme by hyper-rationalists who believe that schools are infinitely manipulable, and at the other extreme by romantic decentralists who believe that if left alone, schools will flourish. The rationalists' strategy for fixing schools is to create new policies and programs. Teacher and student testing, career ladders, increased graduation requirements, master teachers and longer school seat time are some of the palliatives for remedying the ills of schools. The romantic decentralists, on the other hand, believe that relief from stultifying mediocrity lies in deregulation and local control of schools.

The lesson from the states' recent experience with educational reform is that neither the rationalist nor the decentralist strategy is likely to lead to serious improvement in the quality of schooling in America. Texas thought that it could 'manage' school reform by changing the state's administrative structure and promulgating painstakingly prescriptive regulations. But reformers found it difficult to fit even one program, the teacher career ladder, to the needs of teachers in over 1000 school districts. California policy-makers believed that, with the proper fiscal incentives and minimum of regulations, a hundred flowers would bloom in the gardens of school reform. However, California, schools have been more responsive to local needs and pressures than to the desires of state policy-makers.

There is no doubt that both strategies can demonstrate some signs of success. Schools can be cajoled, pressured and intimidated to improve. And certainly, schools can show improvements in test scores; they can increase instructional time and force more students into college preparatory programs. But most of that improvement is likely to be only on paper. If reform is to succeed in a meaningful way, schools have to change the way they do business. Policy-makers must help them make that change.

If policies further fragment schools, it will be harder, not easier, for them to do their work. If reforms further complicate life in the schools, they will remain disconnected from improved educational quality. Implementation of the state-wide career ladder in Texas, for example, became just another program to implement at the district level. It became a source of anxiety and frustration, hardly the motivating tool for teachers that policy-makers had hoped it would be. In California, the reform provisions tended to rubber stamp what was already going on in schools.

Central to school reform is the fact that centralized policy-makers have a limited repertoire from which to draw. They *can* manage what they control. States may control macro-policy — funding, curricular frameworks, teacher certification, textbook selection and the like — but have limited direct control over the daily operation of schools. Consequently, state efforts to manage school improvement represent only one, albeit most visible, dimension of school reform. Two other manifestations of betterment, though less apparent, are equally important.[1]

The first dimension of the overall reform effort might be called the *authorized* movement. This is the world of state mandates, legislation and the highly visible political activity surrounding formal structures and directives. This is the official version of reform. It comprises state efforts to 'manage' educational excellence. Controlling teacher training and evaluation, allocating resources, and specifying curriculum content are some ways that states attempt to manage the process and substance of schooling. We have focused on the authorized movement because it is the most visible response to *A Nation at Risk*.[2] It has received the greatest amount of public attention, and it is where the national reform effort has landed.

The second dimension of the school reform movement might be called the *regional* or *localist* movement. This comprises the blizzard of local and regional activities. It represents local interpretations and responses to the official version of reform. Like the authorized movement, it is structural and regulatory, but its various changes are masked by their dispersion. It is in this morass that projects like the Bay Area Writing Project in California and Theodore Sizer's Coalition of Essential Schools are rooted. Understanding the dimensions of this set of initiatives and the directions in which they are moving on a local, much less national, level is extremely difficult. That does not mean that localism is unimportant. Indeed, it may be far more important than the authorized version. This is the principal, though not sole, arena that state reforms aim to manage. It is also at this level that the sabotage or fudging or redirecting of the centrally proposed and authorized measures takes place.

Local responses to the call for school improvement are highly varied due to the diverse political and social cultures in which they occur. State initiated reforms are shaped locally to conform, with varying degrees of fidelity, to the intentions of centralized policy-makers as they are transformed into school district practice. Local pressures for change, local capacity to act and competing demands on the system are factors that color this movement. This level of reform is influenced by school district budgets and political agendas. In California, the most visible manifestation of this movement is State Superintendent of Public Instruction Bill Honig's mobilization of an informal and unofficial network of schools engaged in educational improvement. The success of California's reform effort is more closely tied to Honig's ability to mobilize local efforts than it is to the specific provisions of the legislation.

The local reform movement comprises more than idiosyncratic responses to state mandates. Locally initiated reform efforts comprise a critical element of this dimension of school improvement. Local and regional innovation and experimentation with curricula, programs and organizational structures is nothing new. The Phoenix school district in Arizona has developed new programs to combat truancy and school drop-outs. In the Millbrae school district in California, principals are evaluated on their clinical supervision skills. Mastery learning and teaching, alternative schools and time on task are fixed features in many schools and became so through local initiative. This dimension can be mobilized, as Bill Honig demonstrates, but cannot be coerced. Regulations and mandates will not compel innovation. Accomplishing that necessitates an entirely different set of state strategies.

The third dimension of reform might simply be called the *conversation*. Perhaps it is best regarded as the *zeitgeist* of reform. It is synonymous with the change in the rhetoric of schooling and thus the attitudes of those who speak. 'Coaching' and 'clinical supervision' have become ubiquitous terms in educational circles. On the national level this aspect of the reform effort was powerfully affected by the purple rhetoric ('a rising tide of mediocrity', 'unilateral disarmament' and 'a nation at risk') of the National Commission on Excellence in Education. On the local level the *conversation* is what teachers talk about in the teachers' room in the wake of *A National at Risk* or the

Carnegie report on teaching. How do teachers and administrators talk about reform, and what do they think about state initiatives to improve educational quality? How do teachers think about career ladder programs or teacher competency testing? The conversation is influenced by various factors: the professional organizations to which teachers and administrators belong, the professional norms teachers develop in schools of education, and how teachers think about themselves and their roles as teachers.[3] How teachers talk about school improvement colors what they do in the classroom. That, in turn, powerfully influences the success or failure of efforts to realize educational excellence. The enormous impact of the *conversation* should not be overlooked in assessing the educational excellence movement. It is also important to recognize the role of professional organizations in directing the conversation. In California, the California Federation of Teachers is experimenting with a concept called 'policy trust agreements', models for collegial decision making in the schools.[4]

Successful reform strategies will integrate the three levels of the reform movement. They proceed simultaneously along each, because the elements are interdependent and mutually reinforcing. The *authorized* dimension defines state interest and expectations and allocates resources to realize them. The *localist* dimension defines implementation and practice. The latter can stimulate change — or resistance to it. Local opposition to state mandated reform in Texas illustrates the inability of state action to override local practice. California, on the other hand, illustrates the effects of a state strategy that relies on local initiative without defining a state role. Local responses to state intent become opportunistic.

A recurring theme of this investigation is the intersection of state strategies with organizational and individual incentives and capacities — the intersection of the three dimensions of reform. In Texas, H. Ross Perot tried deliberately to circumvent what he saw as parochial forces and ignored the importance of the conversation. Consequently, school reform in Texas may take root in local practice, but only because the state education agency is beginning to fill the gaping cracks left open by Perot. Like Bill Honig in California, the state board of education in Texas is seeking ways to mobilize and influence local practice, to bring it in line with state school improvement efforts. South Carolina's strategy, on the other hand, was to initiate reform on all three levels. The process allowed teachers, parents, administrators and students to make state policy goals their own. In retrospect, one of the most important effects of state reform in South

Carolina was to mobilize both the localist movement and the conversation.

State-level policy-makers, professional organizations, schools of education, teachers, administrators and local school officials play important roles in producing a creative tension among the authorized, localist and conversational dimensions of reform. They coexist in uneasy harmony, much more like a John Cage composition than a Johann Sebastian Bach orchestration. Tension among the three is both inevitable and necessary. The fragility of the relationship results from efforts to balance state intent with local initiative and innovation. Domination by the state can stifle both. On the other hand, local responses to reform must occur within a framework of state design.

Developing A Theory of Institutional Support

The lessons from the current wave of state reform efforts indicate that a major shift in policy needs to occur. Policy-makers must focus attention to making schools better places in which to work and generally more satisfying places for those who are associated with them. Though there is no formula for achieving this, there is a theoretical basis for improving the organizational competence of schools.

A theory of institutional support is based on several premises. Chief among them is the proposition that schools as institutions — not teachers or students or curricula — are the principal targets of reform. Tightening curriculum standards and ratcheting up teacher certification requirements, for example, may mean nothing if schools lack the competence to make use of improved curriculum and better qualified teachers. Quality education comes from sound public institutions, not disparate programs. Packaging more and more programs in response to specific educational problems, the strategy of the past twenty years, is a failed strategy. A lesson from the past that present reformers should heed is that institutional culture cannot be circumvented. High quality educational programs cannot exist in unhealthy institutions.

There must also be a clear delineation of authority and responsibility among those who shape the institutional character of schools. State-level policy-makers, local school officials, teachers, administrators, professional organizations figure significantly in creating and maintaining an uneasy tension among the authorized, the localist and the conversational dimension of reform. The three dimensions, in turn, are the requisite elements for creating an organizational culture that promotes educational excellence. Reform can succeed if the three elements combine to foster schools that are purposive and have the flexibility and competence to allocate and use resources to the best advantage.

Authority and responsibility have to be distributed and differentiated across the entire system of education. The states have the responsibility to establish clear expectations and a general educational framework. States provide the resources and create the context in which schools can take shape. Educational policy in most states is a hodgepodge of requirements and regulations. Much of it is shaped anecdotally and incrementally, in response to some success or horror story, or to please a favored interest group. Because it seemed like a good idea to require mandatory counselling of 10th-graders in California, lawmakers included that provision in Senate Bill 813. Good ideas, however, sometimes fall short of becoming good public policy. The state provides $20 per student in the 10th grade. The average three-year high school has 250 10th-graders. That number of students generates $5,000 — perhaps 25 per cent of the compensation of a guidance counselor. Does anyone seriously believe that adding 0.25 FTEs to high schools can have any plausible impact?

It is not enough to simply give schools more autonomy; encouragement and support must come from the larger context of the state. States can specify what body of knowledge students should master by the time they graduate from high school. South Carolina, for example, requires schools to plan, specifies what areas must be addressed in their plans, and holds them accountable for their results. Taking this policy view, however, requires that schools have time to develop and mature organizationally. State policy-makers like to see instant results for which they can take credit or assign blame; they regularly pull schools up by their roots to see how they are doing.

Authority at the local level needs to be decentralized at the school site. A theory of institutional support is anchored in the conviction that everyone in schools is responsible for planning, budgeting and program evaluation. Budgets are tied to assessment and diagnosis: targeting money where it is most needed. Responsibility is not segmented and parcelled out among a host of players in the educational process. For schools to take responsibility for their efficacy means that schools must behave like organizations rather than a conglomeration of related activity centers or a shopping mall. In order to rebuild their institutional coherence, schools must also exercise authority by affirming the fundamental worth of education in everything they do. Hence, teachers, not students, should determine what a school's course offering should be. The authority of schools must also be predicated on the belief that there is a body of knowledge that is worth teaching. That belief must form the organizational and intellectual base on which schools are structured.

Finally, policy-makers and practitioners should focus on what excellent schools do and how they go about it, for it is not merely the resources that schools have but how they use them. Just having highly qualified teachers is not enough. How those teachers fit into the organizational life of schools is what matters. The important question is not what effective schools look like, but what they do that makes them different from other schools.

An important way in which effective schools are different is in their capacity to integrate the elements that comprise schools. Presently, teachers think of themselves as responsible for a certain number of students in a classroom. Teachers are not expected to assume responsibility for the entire school, especially not for long-range planning. Organizational cultures are built on participatory decision-making, planning, goal setting, and problem solving. Professional norms and teacher attitudes are shaped by the workplace, professional organizations and teacher training programs. Before teachers can be expected to take on broader responsibilities, they must be socialized to assume those responsibilities and must be taught the skills to carry them out. Schools of education and professional organizations are the obvious agents to promote this element of educational reform.

Educational policy-makers might look to other organizational models for guidance in building a theory of institutional support. Hospitals are one model. Physicians know that the quality of a patient's hospital care is not limited to the quality of the immediate relationship between the physician and the patient. It is influenced as well by the organizational coherence of the hospital — nurses, dietitians, X-ray and medical technicians, pharmacists, administrators, and maintenance workers play mutually supporting roles in defining the quality of hospital care. The same can be said of schools. While much attention has been paid to the absence of a theory of instructional technology, surprisingly little attention has focused on efforts to develop a theory of institutional support and development.

Our theory of institutional support is meant to serve as a guidepost to policy-makers. It is not intended as a set of prescriptions; that would be the subject of another book. The theory proposes that educational excellence is impossible in the absence of sound, healthy institutions in which to flourish. A way to nurse schools back to health is to help them forge a sense of organizational coherence and purpose. Achieving that may require major restructuring. Perhaps the present school district structure should be replaced by smaller, organizationally more coherent structures, where a single organization includes a high school, and feeder middle and elementary schools. Certainly, building and sustaining an organizational culture would make new and different demands on teachers' and administrators' time. Planning and evaluation would take on greater significance and would command more attention than the three or four days most schools now devote to it. In the end, the reshaped school culture will determine if the reform wave has any impact. Reform is possible only if policy-makers focus their attention to improving the organizational health of schools.

Notes

1. We are indebted to Theodore Sizer in the formulation of the various dimensions of reform. (Correspondence, 15 August 1986).
2. The National Commission on Excellence in Education *A Nation at Risk: The Imperative for Educational Reform*, (April, 1983).
3. See Mary Metz, *Classrooms and Corridors*, (Berkeley, CA.: University of California Press, 1978).
4. Douglas E. Mitchell and Charles T. Kerchner, 'Policy Trust Agreements', *Policy Briefs*, No. 3, Winter 1986 (San Francisco, CA: Far West Laboratory)

Bibliography

Austin-American Statesman, 14 May 1985.

BARDACH, Eugene *The Implementation Game*, (Cambridge, Mass: MIT Press, 1977).

BEDNAR, William C. Jr., 'A survey of the Texas reform package: House Bill 72', *St. Mary's Law Journal*, 16 (1985).

BELLAH, Robert, MADSEN, Richard, SULLIVAN, William M., SWIDLER, Ann, TIPTON, Steven M., *Habits of the Heart: Individualism and Commitment in American Life*, (Berkeley, CA: University of California Press, 1985).

BENVENISTE, Guy, 'Implementation and intervention strategies', in David L. KIRP and Donald N. JENSEN, (Eds) *School Days, Rule Days* (London: Palmer Press, 1986).

BERMAN, Paul 'From compliance to learning: Implementing legally induced reforms,' in David L. KIRP and Donald N. JENSEN, (Eds) *School Days, Rule Days*, (London: Falmer Press, 1986).

BERMAN, Paul and MCLAUGHLIN, Milbery W. *Federal Programs Supporting Educational Change: Vol. VIII*, (Santa Monica, CA: Rand Corp., 1978).

BERMAN, Paul and WEILER, Dan *Improving Student Performance in California*, (Berkeley, CA: California Business Roundtable, 1983).

BOYER, Ernest L. *High School: A Report on Secondary Education in America*, (New York: Harper and Row, 1983).

BLOUGH, William J. 'Governing South Carolina's public schools', Charlie B. TYER and Cole Blease GRAHAM Jr. (Eds) *Local Government in South Carolina: Volume II, The Governmental Landscape*, (Columbia, SC: Bureau of Governmental Research and Service, University of South Carolina, 1985).

CALIFORNIA STATE DEPARTMENT OF EDUCATION 'Performance Report for California Schools: Indicators of Quality', (1985).

CALIFORNIA STATE LEGISLATURE *Analysis of the Budget Bill: A Report of the Joint Budget Committee, 1984–85.* (Sacramento: Office of the Legislative Analyst, 1984).

Cal-Tax News, (Sacramento, CA: California Tax Foundation. 15 June, 1985).

COHEN, David K. 'Reforming school politics', *Harvard Education Review*, 48 (1978).

COHEN, David K. and MURNANE, Richard 'The merits of merit pay', *Public Interest*, 80 (Summer 1985).

COHEN, Michael 'Instructional management and social conditions in effective schools', in Allan ODDEN and L. Dean WEBB (Eds) *School Finance and School Improvement: Linkages in the 1980s*, (Washington, DC: American Education Finance Association, 1983).

COMMITTEE FOR ECONOMIC DEVELOPMENT 'Investing in our children'. Quoted in *Education Week*, 11 September 1985.

CORNETT, Lynn and WEEKS, Karen 'Career ladder plans: Trends and emerging issues — 1985'. *Career Ladder Clearinghouse*, (Atlanta, GA: Southern Regional Education Board, July 1985).

CUBAN, Larry 'School reform by remote control: SB 813 in California', *Phi Delta Kappan*, (November 1984).

CUBAN, Larry 'Transforming the frog into a prince: Effective schools research, policy and practice at the district level', *Harvard Education Review*, 54 (1984).

DOYLE, Dennis P. and FINN, Chester E. Jr. 'American schools and the future of local control', *Public Interest*, 77 (Fall 1984).

DOYLE, Dennis P. and HARTLE, Terry W. *Excellence in Education: The States Take Charge* (Washington, DC: American Enterprise Institute, 1985).

Education Week, 15 January, 1985.

Education Week, 8 May, 1985.

Education Week, 4 September, 1985.

Education Week, 11 September, 1985.

Education Week, 8 January, 1986.

ELMORE, Richard F. 'Backward Mapping: Implementation research and policy decisions', *Political Science Quarterly*, 94 (1979–80).

ELMORE, 'Organizational models of social program implementation', *Public Policy*, 26 (Spring 1978)

ELMORE, Richard F. and MCLAUGHLIN, Milbrey W. 'Strategic choice in federal education policy: The compliance assistance trade-off', in Ann LIEBERMANN and Milbrey W. MCLAUGHLIN (Eds) *Policy-making in Education*, (Chicago: University of Chicago Press, 1982).

FAIRBANKS, Robert and BOECK, Rick 'Reform is here for schools, but are schools ready for reform?' *California Journal*, (October 1983).

FULLER, Lon *The Morality of Law*, (New Haven: Yale University Press, 1964).

GERSTEIN, Robert 'The practice of fidelity to the law', in Samuel KRISLOV *et al.* (Eds) *Compliance and the Law: A Multi-Disciplinary Approach*, (Beverly Hills, CA: Sage Publications 1972).

GOODLAD, John I. *A Place Called School*, (New York: McGraw-Hill 1984).

GRUBB, W. Norton *et al.*, *The Initial Effects of House Bill 72 on Texas Public Schools: The Challenge of Equity and Effectiveness*, (Austin: Lyndon B. Johnson School of Public Affairs, The University of Texas, 1985).

GUTHRIE, James W. and ZUSMAN, Ami *Mathematics and Science Teachers Shortages: What Can California Do?* (Berkeley: Institute of Governmental Studies, University of California, 1982).

HADLEY, Connie 'School calendar', *ECS Clearinghouse Notes*, (Denver, Colo: Education Commission of the States, July 1984).

HERRING, Pendelton *The Politics of Democracy*, (New York: W.W. Norton, 1940).

HILL, Paul T. 'Enforcement and Informal Pressure in the Management of

Federal Categorical Programs in Education'. (Santa Monica, CA: Rand Corp., 1979).

HIPPLE, Theodore H. '"Vivids" and portfolios do not a master teacher make', *Education Week* (19 June, 1985).

HOROWITZ, Donald L. *The Courts and Social Policy*, (Washington, DC: Brookings Institution, 1977).

KADISH, Sanford and KADISH, Mortimer *Discretion to Disobey: A Study of Lawful Departures from Legal Rules*, (Stanford: Stanford University Press, 1973).

KAGAN, Robert A *Regulatory Justice: Implementing a Wage-Price Freeze* (New York: Russell Sage Foundation, 1978).

KAGAN, Robert A 'Regulating business, regulating schools: The problem of regulatory unreasonableness', in David L. KIRP and Donald N. JENSEN, (Eds) *School Days, Rule Days*, (London: Falmer Press, 1986).

KAYE, Loren, *Making the Grade? Assessing School District Progress on SB 813*, (Sacramento, CA: California Tax Foundation 1985).

KIRP, David L. and JENSEN, Donald N., (Eds) *School Days, Rule Days*, (London: Falmer Press, 1986).

The Knoxville News-Sentinel, 30 June, 1985.

LIEBERMAN, Ann and MILLER, Lynne *Teachers, Their World and Their Work: Implications for School Improvement* (Alexandria, VA: Association for Supervision and Curriculum Development 1984).

LIGHTFOOT, Sara Lawrence *The Good High School* (New York: Basic Books, 1983).

LINDBLOOM, Charles E. *Politics and Markets: The World's Political-Economic System* (New York: Basic Books 1977).

LITTLE, Judith Warren *School Success and Staff Development: The Role of Staff Development in Urban Desegregated Schools* (Washington, DC: National Institute of Education, 1981).

LORTI, Dan C, *Schoolteacher: A Sociological Study*, (Chicago: University of Chicago Press, 1975).

LOWI, Theodore J, *The End of Liberalism*, (New York: Norton, 1969).

MADDOX, Peggy 'Testing Arkansas teachers: The "Quick-Fix" politics of reform', *Education Week*, 11 September, 1985.

McLAUGHLIN, W. MILBREY, *et al.*, 'State policy and teaching excellence'. (Standford, CA: Institute for the Study of Educational Finance and Governance, School of Education, Forthcoming).

MERTON, Robert K, *Social Theory and Social Structures*, (New York: The Free Press, 1957).

METZ, Mary *Classrooms and Corridors,* (Berkeley, CA.: University of California Press, 1978)

MEYER, John 'Organizational factors affecting legalization', in David L. KIRP, and Donald N. JENSEN, (Eds) *School Days, Rule Days,* (London: Falmer Press 1986).

MEYER, John W., SCOTT, Richard, STRANG, David and CREIGHTON, Andrew. 'Bureaucratization without centralization: Changes in the organizational system of American public education, 1940–1980'. (Stanford, CA: Institute for Research on Educational Finance and Governance, August 1985).

MITCHELL, Douglas 'State policy strategies for improving teacher quality', *Policy Briefs* Number 1 (San Francisco: Far West Laboratory for Educational Research and Development, 1986).

MITCHELL, Douglas and KERCHNER, Charles T. 'Policy trust agreements', *Policy Briefs* Number 3 (San Francisco: Far West Laboratory for Educational Research and Development, 1987)

MUIR, William Kerr *Police: Streetcorner Politicians*, (Chicago: University of Chicago Press, 1977).

NATIONAL CENTER FOR EDUCATION STATISTICS. *Bulletin* (US Department of Education, Office of the Assistant Secretary for Educational Research and Improvement, July 1984).

THE NATIONAL COMMISSION ON EXCELLENCE IN EDUCATION *A Nation at Risk: The Imperative for Educational Reform*, (Washington, DC: US Department of Education. April 1983).

NEA REPORTER *A Closer Look at Teacher Education,* (Washington, DC: National Education Association, 1982).

NEAL, David and KIRP, David L. 'The allure of legalization reconsidered: The case of special education', in David L. KIRP and Donald N. JENSEN (Eds) *School Days, Rule Days*, (London: Falmer Press 1986).

Newsweek, 'Help wanted: Teachers', 9 September, 1986.

New York Times, 'Education survey', Spring 1985.

New York Times, 23 May, 1985.

NONET, Philippe and SELZNICK, Phillip *Law and Society in Transition: Toward Responsive Law*, (New York: Harper and Row, 1978).

NORTON, John 'Our Schools, A Special Report', *The State* (Columbia, SC: Part I, 15 January, 1984; Part II, 22 January, 1984; Part III, 29 January, 1984).

ODDEN, Allan and DOUGHERTY, Van *State Programs of School Improvement: A 50-State Survey*, (Denver: Education Commission of the States, 1982).

Parade, 1 December, 1986.

PASSOW, A. Harry *Reforming Schools in the 1980s: A Critical Review of the National Reports* (New York: Clearinghouse on Urban Education, Teachers College, Columbia University, 1984).

POWELL, Arthur G, FARRAR, Eleanor and COHEN, David K. *The Shopping Mall High School*, (Boston: Houghton Mifflin, 1985).

PRESSMAN, Jeffrey and WILDAVSKY, Aaron *Implementation*, (Berkeley: University of California Press, 1973).

PURKEY, Stewart and SMITH, Marshall 'Effective schools — A review', *Elementary School Journal*, 83 (1983).

RAVITCH, Diane *The Troubled Crusade: American Education 1945–1980*, (New York: Basic Books, 1983).

RHEINSTEIN, Max (Ed.) *Max Weber on Law in Economy and Society*, (New York: Simon and Schuster, 1967).

RUTTER, Michael *et al.*, *Fifteen Thousand Hours: Secondary Schools and Their Effects on Children*, (Cambridge, Mass: Harvard Press, 1979).

SCHATTSCHNEIDER, E.E. *The Semisovereign People*, (Hinsdale, Ill: Dryden Press, 1960).

SCHRAG, Peter 'School reform: The neglected agenda', *Sacramento Bee*, 25 September, 1985.

SCHULTZE, Charles *The Public Use of Private Interest*, (Washington, DC: Brookings Institution, 1977).

SELECT COMMITTEE ON PUBLIC EDUCATION, 'Recommendations' (Austin, TX: State Printing Office, 19 April, 1984).

SHULMAN, Judith, ST. CLAIR, George and LITTLE, Judith Warren *Expanded Teacher Roles: Mentors and Masters*, (San Francisco: Far West Laboratory for Education Research and Development 1984).

SILBER, John R. 'Higher education in the United States'. Japanese-United States Conference on Higher Education, Drew University, Madison, NJ 7 August, 1985).

SIZER, Theodore R. *Horace's Compromise: The Dilemma of the American High School*, (Boston: Houghton Mifflin 1985).

SOUTH CAROLINA Office of the Governor and State Department of Education. 'The public viewpoint: Education in South Carolina', (1983).

STODDARD, Trish, LOSK, David J and BENSON, Charles 'Some reflections on the honorable profession of teaching'. (Berkeley: University of California, Policy Analysis for California Education, Graduate School of Education, 1984).

TASK FORCE ON EDUCATION FOR ECONOMIC GROWTH *Action in the States: Progress Toward Educational Renewal*, (Denver, Colo: Education Commission of the States, 1984).

TEXAS STATE LEGISLATURE *Texas House Journal* (68th Legislature, Second Called Session, 5 June, 1984).

TOCH, Thomas 'The dark side of the excellence movement'. *Phi Delta Kappan*, (November 1984).

TYACK, David B. *The One Best System*, (Cambridge, Mass: Harvard Press, 1974).

US DEPARTMENT OF EDUCATION *The Nation Responds: Recent Efforts to Improve Education*, (Washington, DC: Government Printing Office, 1984).

VERSTEGEN, Deborah A., HOOKER, Richard and ESTES, Nolan 'A comprehensive shift in educational policy-making: Texas education reform legislation', in *The Fiscal, Legal, and Political Aspects of State Reform of Elementary and Secondary Education*, (San Francisco, CA: Ballinger, 1986).

Washington Post, 4 September, 1984.

WEATHERLY, Richard and LIPSKY, Michael 'Street-level bureaucrats and institutional innovation: Implementing special education reform', *Harvard Education Review*, 47 (1977).

WHITE, Merry 'Japanese education: How do they do it?' *The Public Interest*, 76 (Summer 1974).

WILDAVSKY, Aaron *Speaking Truth to Power: The Art and Craft of Policy Analysis*, (Boston: Little, Brown and Co., 1979).

WISE, Arthur E. *Legislated Learning: The Bureaucratization of the American Classroom*, (Berkeley: University of California Press, 1979).

Index